Advance praise for H

"Fragmented yet unified, direct yet elusive, *How to Walk with Steve* is a vivid memoir about family and geography, obligation and freedom. Fromberg has a remarkable ability to inject meaning into silence, into the cracks between sections, into all the things that remain unsaid."
  –Brett Biebel, author of *48 Blitz*

"*How to Walk with Steve* is an inviting, conversational, and deeply personal portrait of a man's relationship with his brother across places and across time. Full of humor, honesty, and surprise, Fromberg's carefully crafted memoir shows the challenges and obligations—and also the faith and love—that connect siblings through the years."
  –Scott Kenemore, author of *Lake of Darkness*

"Fully aware of his brother's oblique brilliance as well as his most upsetting tics, Fromberg presents the string of decisions, unforced errors, and well-meaning efforts that he made along the way to adulthood. He is as unsparing to himself as he is to those around him, and the effect is both agonizing and hilarious."
  –Valerie Block, author of *Was It Something I Said?*

"Robert Fromberg's poignant memoir details the painful ordinariness of misery—even for the bright scion of an artistic family.

The narrator's experience of the Peoria landscape with its dull roads and trains and repetitive residential streets—and of jobs that involve repeated tasks—echo the description of Steve's obsessions and compulsions. In this way, Fromberg normalizes Steve's behavior and brings him fully into the range of common experience. Over time, the writer grows beyond merely accepting responsibility for his brother; he comes to cherish him and the irreducible bond the brothers share when all else is stripped away. In refusing easy consolations, Fromberg has created a memoir that shines like polished bone."

–Patricia Eakins, author of *The Hungry Girls and Other Stories*

"Without a trace of affectation or adornment, Fromberg depicts the searing moments that made him who he is. Never have I read a more authentic, deeply-felt rendering of a child's developing mind."

–Leslie Lawrence, author of *The Death of Fred Astaire: And Other Essays from a Life Outside the Lines*

How to *Walk* with Steve

How to
Walk with
Steve

A memoir

Robert Fromberg

Pieces of this book, most in very different forms, previously appeared in
*Anti-Heroin Chic, The Bitchin' Kitsch, Burnt Breakfast, Callosum, Drunk
Monkeys, Foliate Oak Literary Review, 45th Parallel, HASH, Hobart,
Indiana Review, Local Honey Midwest, The Tennessee Quarterly,* and
VERSIFICATION.

Book and cover design by Kevin Breen

ISBN: 978-1-7360127-2-7
Cataloging-in-Publication Data is available upon request

Manufactured in the United States of America

Published by
Latah Books, Spokane, Washington
www.latahbooks.com

The author may be contacted at robertfrombergwriter.com

For Sheryl

About twenty-five years ago, a college student of mine asked to interview me for a project she was doing for another class. I liked this student. She was a terrific writer and had a sharp tongue. I wanted to impress her.

We met in a coffee shop. She said, "OK, tell me your life story."

For me, the perfect question.

I told her that I was born in Peoria, Illinois, that my mother and father were both artists, that my mother was an alcoholic and a sleeping pill addict, and that I had an autistic brother I took care of a lot as we were growing up. I told her that I started college at age 15, that at age 16 I moved to New York City by myself, that my Dad, only 52, died a couple of years later, and that I returned home. I told her that my mom died soon after, that I became my autistic brother's guardian, that I got married, that the three of us moved to North Carolina to get my brother proper care, that I started teaching college at age 23, that my wife divorced me soon after, and that I moved to Chicago and still take care of my brother.

Finished with my answer, I settled back to await her praise.

She looked up from her notebook, and said, "That's it?"

1959-1971

My mother is running from our front door to the car in the driveway, holding the baby and screaming. My dad tells the rest of us to get into the car. I think that I am moving too slowly, I am delaying our departure, I am making the situation worse. As we near the hospital door and Dad begins to slow the car, Mom jumps out with the baby and runs the rest of the way, screaming and crying.

✦

Each day in the late morning, my mother makes a sandwich, sets the plate on the kitchen table, and covers the sandwich with a ceramic bowl. The process feels brittle and silent. My dad comes home, sits alone at the kitchen table, eats the sandwich, then stands and says he is "heading back to school." I am happy that my dad has this sandwich each day, under a bowl with beautiful texture, quiet, alone.

*

My little brother, Steve, does not talk. But he runs. He runs from room to room. He runs inside his room. When he sits, he bounces. That is the word we use. He leans forward, lets his back fall into the seat, bounces forward, falls back, bounces forward. I try to bounce. It feels good, like sleeping in motion.

1

*

Each afternoon, my mother announces to me that it is "apple and orange time." She brings a basket with apples and oranges, and a book. I like oranges better than apples, and I pick one. My mother begins reading. I am fully aware of what is happening. My mother is luring me to eat fruit because fruit is good for me. She wants to be sure that I eat fruit once each day. She lures me with the festive-sounding "apple and orange time." She lures me with the book. Each day at apple and orange time, we sit on the couch, and I feel a wall in front of the couch, an invisible wall, between my mom and me and the book and our apples and oranges, and a path that would lead me away. This time of day begins the bad time of day. The time when I cry and when I want my dad to come home.

Today, while my mother reads, I toss the orange back and forth between my hands. I roll it between my palms. Its surface is entrancing. Its weight is perfect. Also, I am able to move my hands and arms rather than sit still, as I know my mother prefers. I think I have solved the problem of apple and orange time; I have found a way not to feel constrained. Mom has not noticed—or at least not commented on—my movements, which shocks me, because Mom seems to notice everything, and when she does, she uses her word: "inappropriate." Or her phrase: "What would your grandfather think?" Or her other phrase: "You won't get into Yale if you behave that way." My mom stops reading and reaches her hand out for the orange so she can peel it. When she grasps the orange, she looks at me. She squeezes the orange. I watch her thin hand, her thin wrist. "It's ruined," she says. She looks at me. I have made her angry and I have also helped to break her.

*

My mother is standing in our front yard, talking with a neighbor. That my mother is standing in the front yard is unusual. That she is talking with a neighbor is astonishing. I approach.

"They left a month ago," the neighbor is saying. She gestures toward the yellow house across the street. "They left in the middle of the night. The man was"—here the neighbor's enunciation becomes more studied—"being pursued."

"Oh?" my mother says, not seeming terribly interested.

The neighbor looks at my mother squarely, then squints as though my mother emanates some bright and unpleasant light.

"You just hide behind your trees," the neighbor says. "You don't know what's happening right across the street from you."

The neighbor pauses, seeming satisfied at having had this opportunity to say something that has needed saying for a long time.

That night, I imagine the family in the yellow house on the night they fled. Late in the evening, the father told the mother and the little girl that they had to leave within the hour. Their car filled rapidly with their possessions. The girl was allowed only to take things she could hold in her lap. Her chest seemed ready to tear open from mourning the things she couldn't take and from fear over where they were going, but she saw the expression on her father's face and said nothing. Her father told her to stay in the house until he gave her the signal. When he did, she moved quickly to the car. He followed her and seemed to shut the house and car doors carefully, as though not wanting anyone to hear.

*

Sitting in the window seat, looking through the picture window that dominates the small room, what I mostly see are needles and branches of evergreen trees. I know that outside, the needles that gather under the evergreen trees are a wonderfully bouncy cushion. They are only sharp if you touch them at the wrong angle.

*

I ask my dad again to read me the liner notes of the movie soundtrack album to West Side Story. We are lying on the living room rug. He opens the album gatefold and lays it on the rug. While he reads, I look at the pictures in the gatefold. Young men in tennis shoes, on their toes, flinging their legs and arms out, out, out. They may fly away they are so full of confidence and joy and wholeness, ready to fly in front of a row of apartments. And people dead. Riff is lying on his face. I try to will him to move again and know I cannot. I stare at the finality of his position, the drama, drama that equals death. Bernardo, also stabbed, lying on his side. He is harder to see, his position looks more comfortable. I try to instill his death in myself.

Tony shot, falling into Maria's arms, night in a playground, not falling, collapsing, she is holding him up, she loves him, and he is suddenly dead. Another picture of Tony dead, lying on his back, in profile, his lips parted, speaking ended. I ask my dad to read the story again. I go back to the tennis shoe toes, the uplifted feet, the wildly outstretched arms. I have never seen a body express anything like that.

*

My parents and we boys—my big brother, Paul, my little brother, Steve, and I—leave Peoria for New York City. Mom and Dad say that for six months we will live in an apartment building on East 88th Street. Those words, "88th Street," sound like a ball bouncing.

Paul goes to first grade in a school that doesn't have a name, only the letters P.S. followed by a number. A school with a name that is a number makes me feel small and overwhelmed, and I feel bad that my brother needs to go there. I am told that I am too young for kindergarten, so my mother and I go some days to a park where there is concrete and benches but no grass, but where there is a group of other children.

Inside the street door of our apartment are two columns of buttons, a name beside each. Towering columns of buttons. I can reach only the bottom few rows, but our apartment's button is toward the top, or so I am told, because I don't know how to read, even our name.

My father puts a small wooden folding stool with a red seat in the vestibule so I can reach the button, and he paints our button red so I can identify it. I am familiar with the stroke of Dad's painting, and I believe I can identify it in the red on the button.

These arrangements are so that I will not be trapped downstairs when I want to come home after being outside, alone.

One day, I enter the vestibule and the stool is gone. I look up at the columns of buttons. I reach up. The red button is beyond my reach.

The vestibule seems darker than usual. There is both a blankness and a vastness to the consequences of this situation. Pieces of scenarios appear and disappear. Waiting in this dark vestibule—for how long? What would waiting for hours be like? Going outside—to go where? Outside are boys who will shout things at me and throw things—they have done it before. Outside to walk somewhere? To the park where I have my morning play group? Could I find the park? The place where my heart is throbs.

I look up at the buttons. Each looks beautiful to me, rounded, I imagine, from a thousand touches from a thousand fingers.

I reach up and push a button.

A woman's crackly "hello" comes through the speaker.

"Hello," I say. "I am a little boy. I live in this building. I'm too small to reach my button. Can you let me in?"

I hear a buzz, and I push the door. As I enter, I believe that I understand something that I did not understand before.

*

Back in Peoria, in kindergarten, people are wearing costumes. I am wearing a cowboy holster. In the holster, I have not a toy pistol, but a toy rifle. The barrel straddles my leg. I have to walk stiff legged. Several kids ask why I don't have a normal costume. Later that day, I tell my mom that I do not want to go back to kindergarten. At some point, my parents tell me I am sick and will not go back to the school, and I am aware that I have left something important incomplete.

*

A wiry, powerful-looking neighbor girl approaches me and says she saw my little brother lean over and lick a pile of dog shit. I know my brother's habits and behaviors. They do not vary. He would not do this. I tell her that, but she ignores me, and I am aware that her will to believe or say or do anything is superior to mine.

*

In our neighborhood on the outskirts of Peoria, every other summer a truck goes once up and once down the long street in front of our house, laying down glittering tar. Another truck goes once up and once down the street, depositing gravel on top of the tar. For weeks after, as our family car drives on the street, I hear the gravel ricocheting off the car's undercarriage. The fact that my family and our neighbors have the task of tamping down the gravel over a several-week period makes me feel that I am part of a tiny, forgotten community.

This is a favorite time for my little brother. He sits in the back of the car, bouncing against the seat back.

*

My brother Steve will only eat toast and jelly, and Carl Buddig brand corned beef with ketchup. When he eats toast and jelly, he picks up the toast, turns it over so the jelly falls in his lap, and then puts it in his mouth.

He will only drink apple juice.

He kneels down and looks along the edges of furniture. I try this too, and it looks dramatic.

My mom has told me these things about Steve: that he had a twin brother who died, that when Steve was a baby, he stopped breathing and had to be rushed to the hospital.

Steve listens to only a few seconds of a record album, then picks up the needle and puts it down in the same spot. He does this many times. I sit in his room with him while he does this.

When the family goes out in public, if I try to hold Steve's hand, he pulls away. If I lose my grasp, he runs away from the family.

When my parents are gone or busy, I sit with Steve while he watches *Sesame Street*. I watch to make sure he doesn't run out of the house.

During the day, he goes to a place where they pin him to the floor and force him to eat foods he does not like.

*

I am with my mother at the five-and-ten-cent store. I see a box containing a model car, the kind you have to build from instructions. I know that having the model car will make me feel good. I also know that—because my mother will not want to spend the money to buy me the model car and if she buys it will do so with annoyance—the model car will make me feel bad.

I tell my mom that I want the model car. I point to it—up on a shelf I can't reach. She says no. I ask again. She looks back and forth—as if to see if anyone is watching—and says yes.

I spend the afternoon in the room I share with my older brother, building the model. When I am finished, I run out of my room, holding the model. As I cross the threshold of my room, I hit the model on the doorframe, and much of it breaks. I begin to cry, hard. My mom approaches and sees the damage.

"If you get sad when I buy you things, then I won't buy you things."

I cry harder, but also I begin to laugh because everything fits, just like the pieces of the model: Everything good is bad.

*

I am in line along a wall of waist-high shelves. Each student in line is holding a pencil. It is the first task of the first day in first grade. Although I assume that the other students in the room live in my neighborhood, I do not recognize any of them. They, however, seem to know each other.

The student at the front of the line is sharpening a pencil in the hand-crank sharpener. I observe carefully, aware I have never been here before, wanting to perform perfectly, wanting not to be spotted as the boy who did not complete kindergarten. The students in line, and those seated who have already sharpened their pencils, poke each other and giggle. Students jostle in line, using the phrase, "No cuts," a phrase they clearly understand but I do not. I recognize that they share habits and language that I do not share. The room's color is defined by the dirt-tan desktops. Time seems impossible—that a day would pass with these students in this dirt-tan room, doing one new thing after another that everyone but me already understands.

A boy seated near the line thrusts his already sharpened pencil toward those in line as they approach him. The boy looks dangerous to me; his thrusts look thoughtless in a way that seems irresponsible. He has an oddly shaped smile. I expect him to do one of two things as I approach: to ignore me, or to stab me in anger. However, when I am near him, he thrusts his pencil toward me in exactly the manner he does toward the others. I even sense that his smile might be friendly, perhaps even friendlier toward me. I am scared of him, but I know that I should respond. This, after all, is what people who are in the group do. They have fun with one another. I thrust my pencil back in his direction, imitating his sword-fight gesture.

"You," the teacher says. She is an older woman, perhaps only a bit younger than my grandmother in New York. She is looking at me. "You boys," she says, now including the other boy in her glance. She accelerates toward us, hands extended, and swipes my pencil out of my hand and then the pencil from my accomplice's hand. "If you can't be responsible, then you can't have pencils."

I understand that the other boy may be a bad boy, and that the teacher has put me in the group with him. My chest feels as if it is opening and swallowing me. My head buzzes. My face radiates heat. I am falling. I know the feeling will never stop. I want everyone to understand that I am a good boy.

*

I understand things without knowing how I understand them. They are things that seem like the walls demarcating the rooms in our house, like the air I sense hovering thick within those walls. I understand things about my dad. I understand that he is sick, although he does not lie in bed like sick people on television. I understand that Dad cannot drink milk. (Instead of milk, he pours a gray-looking mixture of water and something powdered, from a jar with no label, onto his Shredded Wheat.) I understand that he cannot walk in a field in summertime because the things he would breathe would make him sick. I understand that we cannot have a pet with fur, although we can have a turtle.

*

The car is in the driveway. Standing at the front window of our house, I see my mom in the driver's seat. Steve is in the back seat. Although they are in silhouette, I am convinced I can see Mom's face—her expression determined while her face seems to collapse.

As she left the house, she seemed to sweep Steve up. My father stood near the door. A moment before that, she said, "I'm going." I knew she was not going to the store, but that she was going forever.

I watch her back out of the driveway, faster than usual, and turn onto the street that leads to Harmon Highway. I imagine Mom and Steve driving into downtown Peoria. I imagine them driving around the city, my mom trying to think of a place to go. I imagine them leaving the city. I imagine them stopping at a motel.

From the knees down, my legs vibrate. I feel as if I am dissolving, like the Wicked Witch of the West at the end of *The Wizard of Oz*.

I imagine them returning to Peoria—perhaps two years from now—my mom still driving, Steve still in the back seat. I will be standing on a sidewalk downtown and will see them drive by. I am pretty sure my mom will not see me, but even if she does, she will not stop.

At dinnertime, Mom and Steve are home.

*

Sometimes my classmates say, "Sticks and stones will break my bones, but names will never hurt me." When I hear this, I know I do not have to worry because I will be the best boy, and I will never give anyone a reason to call me a bad name.

*

At dinner, my dad takes a bite of food, takes a sip of tea, and coughs. His cough sounds like something has fallen apart in his throat and his chest. My mom, my brothers, and I are quiet. I watch my dad. He takes a bite of food, takes a sip of tea, and coughs. We are supposed to be quiet. But sometimes, like tonight, my brother Paul and I exchange a look or a sound that triggers a giggle between us, and Dad tries to say, "Boys," but is overtaken by coughing—this time longer and fiercer. If we are not quiet, Dad has trouble swallowing. I find that I can eat in five minutes and then ask to be excused from the table.

*

At school, while the class is coloring, a classmate asks me my favorite color. I suspect that the truth would get a reaction that I would not like. My favorite color is ocher. Once I saw a painting on a cover of a magazine at home and pointed to a color in the upper left corner and asked my mom what that color was called, and she said, "Ocher," and the word was as wonderful as the color.

I reply to my classmate that my favorite color is blue.

He glances at my coloring in progress. It features oranges and browns. He says, "I don't see any blue there."

I vow to color in blue from now on.

*

My mother keeps a large cardboard container of cans of Schlitz beer in the closet in her painting studio. I see her bring the containers home with the groceries. I never see her drink these cans of beer.

13

*

James Earl Ray has shot Martin Luther King, Jr. The radio says that James Earl Ray is on the run in the Midwest. Much of the night, I imagine that he is climbing through the tiny windows, positioned high on the walls of my bedroom.

*

In the backyard, Paul and I play Wiffle ball. When you throw a Wiffle ball, the force of the throw has little effect on its speed. How hard you swing the bat has little effect on how far the ball travels. The ball seems to launch and then float, propelled more by air or perhaps whim than anything I have done. Often, I let conventional expectations direct me, and I throw harder and swing harder, with little consequence. But also, I love to throw more softly and to swing more calmly. And most of all, I like the stillness of when the Wiffle ball seems suspended in the air, as though it will hang there forever.

*

My dad used to paint big canvases with huge, solemn brushstrokes. Now he creates what he tells me is called kinetic art. He makes huge boxes painted red and blue that you look inside to see dancing and sliding dots and lines. He makes paintings with wooden slats that turn back and forth and wooden circles that spin. Everything on his kinetic art goes slowly, a little stiffly. I love waiting for each piece to move.

14

*

After dinner, Paul and I are sitting on the living room floor, watching television. Mom and Dad enter together, ask us to turn off the TV and sit on the couch. Mom is holding Steve's hand, and he is pulling away. We sit. Mom and Dad stand facing us.

Dad tells us that he and Mom might get a divorce.

Mom says, "Steve will of course come with me."

I think, what about Dad and Steve? What about me and Steve?

Mom says, "Now, who do you boys want to go with?"

Dad says, "LaVerne, don't force them to choose."

Mom says, "Paul…?"

Paul pauses, then says, "You."

Mom says, "Rob…?"

I look from my mom to my dad. I want to say, Dad. In my stomach, I feel how much I want to say, Dad. I look at my Mom. I know she is weaker than Dad. I know she could break with just a light tap.

I say, "Mom."

I know that I have injured my dad forever.

The next day, we go to school and have dinner and watch TV.

The day after that, we also go to school and have dinner and watch TV.

I watch my dad's eyes.

*

Dad leads Paul and me in a project: staining the redwood siding of our house. I love the weight of the brush and the watery consistency of the stain. It is impossible to make a mistake. I can slather on the stain any way I want with no ill consequences. When we are finished, I can see no difference in the appearance of the redwood siding, but I can see by my dad's face that we have done a good thing. The house is small, and the project does not take long. The air is still.

*

In every issue of *Boys' Life* magazine is an advertisement in the form of a seven-panel cartoon. I always read the first three panels. In the first panel, an unattractively skinny man and a pretty woman sitting on a beach blanket are disturbed by a muscular man with a beach ball who is kicking sand at them. In the second panel, the muscular man threatens the skinny man. In the third panel, the beautiful woman leaves the skinny man. I believe that I understand a central truth from these three panels: The muscular man is part of a group of happy people who play beach ball with each other. If you are not in that group, the person you love will leave you to join that group.

*

My mom and dad say that I talk all the time. My dad says this with a smile. My mom states it like something my teacher would say.

*

We have not yet eaten breakfast, but Steve is sitting in the back seat of our station wagon with his maps beside him. He bounces against the seat back, gazing through the windshield.

Dad has a concentrated look as he arranges suitcases under a tarp on top of the car and blankets and pillows and boxes of food inside the car.

We coax Steve into the house for breakfast, and then we all climb into the car. Paul gets first dibs on stretching out in the station wagon back, Steve resumes his spot and his bouncing in the back seat, I sit beside him, Dad is in the driver's seat, humming as he pulls out of the driveway, and Mom occupies the passenger's seat, leaning against a pillow between her and the window.

As we drive, Steve continues to bounce while observing closely through the windows, except when he consults the map unfolded on his lap.

When darkness comes, we pull into a gas station, and Dad rearranges the contents of the car, making beds for Steve on the back seat, and for Paul and me in the station wagon's back. As he makes the beds, we stand to one side, arms wrapped around ourselves in the chill. Watching Dad create our beds in the car, I want to hug him, but don't. I feel taken care of.

Lying in the back of the station wagon, I don't try to sleep, and I don't try to stay awake. I could listen to the semi-trucks whoosh by forever.

As we get closer to Brooklyn, my dad speaks more than he usually speaks. His voice sounds different, his accent changing to be more like the imitations he does of his parents and aunts and uncles.

Every time we approach a toll booth, Steve bounces harder.

As my dad tosses coins into the toll baskets, he pretends to be a basketball player.

In Brooklyn, the pavement on the streets looks as soft as cake frosting and sleek black. (In Peoria, the pavement is forgettable shades of gray.)

In Brooklyn, the street signs are all black with white letters. (In Peoria, some street signs are white with black letters and some are green with white letters.)

In Brooklyn, there are sidewalks. (In Peoria, we walk in the street.)

In Brooklyn, the houses are all old, close together. near to the curb and alike. (In Peoria, the houses are behind lawns and are of varying shapes and sizes and have nothing that captures the eye and are neither close together nor far apart.)

In Brooklyn, people sit on the porches of their house and talk. (In Peoria, no one is visible.)

In Brooklyn, people walk on the sidewalks and play in the playgrounds. (In Peoria, no one is visible.)

In Brooklyn, people look you in the eye. (In Peoria, they look down.)

In Brooklyn, talk is recreational and loud and continuous—in stores, as you pass on the street, everywhere. (In Peoria, people talk only when they must.)

In Brooklyn, the people look like one large family—olive skin, dark hair. (In Peoria, I don't notice what the people look like.)

When we arrive, Steve whispers to himself, "Brooklyn has black-and-white street signs."

*

My mother's wrists and forearms are thin. Her neck is thin. However, when she grasps a paint brush, her forearm muscles flex. Her brush moves toward the canvas with utter authority. Sometimes she uses a waxy paint that she applies with a palette knife in one hand and a blow torch in the other. She also drags paint over large screens inside wooden frames on top of large canvases with a squeegee that reminds me of a steamroller.

*

On TV, I see Robert Kennedy shot in a crowd. He is running for the 1968 Democratic nomination for president. He is running against Ed Muskie, Hubert Humphrey, and Eugene McCarthy, who is my favorite. Kennedy had just given a speech after winning two state primaries. Kennedy is still alive. I have a thought. It is a horrible thought. It is a thought that I know I will never be able to forget that I have had. It is a thought that makes as a bad person.

The thought is this: If Robert Kennedy dies, Eugene McCarthy, my favorite, will be more likely to be the nominee; therefore, I want Robert Kennedy to die.

The next day, Kennedy dies, and I know that the thought will be with me for the rest of my life.

*

Sometimes I model for my mother, but I know that I am not a good model. She tells me to sit still.

Sometimes I sit with my mom while she paints. Once she is painting my younger brother at a beach onto a huge canvas. She is telling me that she wishes she lived in a cold-water flat in New York City. She did not, she says, plan to be in a place like Peoria. When she says Peoria, her mouth looks like she is tasting something terrible.

*

I love allergist appointments. My dad and I go together to the allergist every week. On the way, I talk with my dad about movies and books. The doctor's examination room has a desk pushed against a wall. My dad and I sit on opposite sides of the desk. The nurse enters and gives my dad one injection in each arm and gives me an injection in one arm. After the nurse leaves, my dad and I joke—very quietly—about how one nurse, named Whinny, gives such painful injections. Then Dad and I read magazines while we wait to see the doctor. After about fifteen minutes, the allergist enters. He is tall and has dark, wild, thinning hair. He limps slightly; my dad once told me that the allergist had polio as a child. The allergist looks like my dad—only taller and more confident. Although people almost never visit our house and although we almost never visit other people's houses, I understand that our family has friends whom we never see socially and that the allergist is one. He and my dad chat for a moment—the allergist's wife acts in local productions and was in one of my dad's experimental films, and the doctor's son is a bluegrass fiddler. As they speak, the allergist feels my dad's arms at the site of the injection for any reaction. Then he turns his chair toward me. I place my forearm on the desk, and the doctor gently grasps my arm, rubbing his thumb lightly on the injection site. I love the feel of his touch. I love that every week, I get to be touched on my skin.

*

The family is watching the television together, something we rarely do. A guitarist is singing a song about the assassinations of Abraham Lincoln, Martin Luther King, Jr., John Kennedy, and Robert Kennedy, one verse devoted to each. In the middle of the song, I realize that an image of each assassinated man is appearing in the lower right corner of the screen. It feels like an important and exciting discovery. "Look," I say, pointing to the screen, "a picture of Martin Luther King."

My mom says, "Let's see if we can enjoy it silently."

*

I wake to murmuring voices, men's voices. I get up, open my bedroom door, and step into the hall. My parents' bedroom door is open. I see men in uniforms, saying my mother's first name to her—which I know that my mother would find inappropriate—and getting no response. They lift her onto a stretcher. Her head and arms flop as they lift her body. I return to my room, close the door, and am surprised that I am able to manufacture tears and an appropriate phrase: "I don't want my mom to die."

The next morning, heavy with dread, I walk downstairs. Mom is sitting alone at the kitchen table. It seems impossible that she could have been taken away limp in an ambulance last night and be home now.

I am not sure what words will be correct. I settle on these: "Do you feel OK?"

She glares at me, says, "Yes," and turns away.

*

My dad takes my older brother and me to a showing of the movie *Duck Soup*. Dad says this is one of his favorite movies, that he loved it as a boy.

On the way home, I cannot stop laughing. My laughing slows until I remember another scene from the movie, and I start laughing again. I am sitting beside my dad in the front seat. He does not try to stop my laughter, even after it has gone on for what I realize must be longer than people usually laugh.

*

Summer evening. The sun is down. A hard rain begins. My mother appears in the living room. "Rain!" She sounds joyful. Her voice bounces in a way I have never heard. "Rain!"

My dad and brothers appear. I take Steve's arm.

"It's beautiful!" my mom says. "Let's go out!"

She opens the door to our backyard. We follow. It is raining hard. I am quickly soaked but am drawn to follow my mother. We all seem to be.

In the backyard, two parts of our roof meet in a V pointing toward the ground, where a bed of rocks receives the runoff. Rain is streaming from the roof.

My mother stands underneath it, waving her arms. She begins taking off her clothes, then her underwear, amazingly graceful and athletic under the streaming water. She stretches out her arms parallel to the ground. She rotates slowly. Rain soaks her hair, streams over her breasts, her stomach, her pubic hair. We watch.

*

My teacher asks the class, "How many of your fathers work at Caterpillar?"

About two thirds of the class members raise their hands.

"How many of your fathers work at Pabst?"

About half the remaining students raise their hands.

"How many of your fathers work at Hiram Walker?"

Several more hands go up.

Eventually, I am asked where my father works. "He works at Bradley University," I say.

"What does he do there?"

"He teaches art," I say.

I cannot explain the large colorful boxes and moving paintings in my house to any classmate who visits. It is safer for me to visit their houses. Those houses have carpet, puffy furniture, pictures of family, smells of cooking, family members milling around the house. However, in those houses, my overwhelming sense is of wanting to leave—not to go any specific place, but to not be there.

*

My mom pulls the car up to the curb in front of the dentist's office. She asks me to go inside and tell the receptionist that I know I missed my appointment; could I get another date and time? My mom says that she will wait in the car.

Inside, I recite my lines to the receptionist. Seated at the counter, she can look me straight in the eye without raising or lowering her head. She holds my eyes a moment, then stands and walks through a doorway. When she returns, she says that the dentist will not make another appointment for my family. I see the dentist in the doorway, frowning, shaking his head.

Back in the car, I report the verdict to my mother. She stiffens, then starts the car and pulls rapidly away from the curb.

*

When we drive through our neighborhood, its roads freshly paved with tar and gravel, Steve says, "Gravel has little rocks in it."

My dad says, cheerfully, "Gravel is little rocks."

Steve says, "Gravel is little rocks!"

*

In class, I sit near the front of the room so that the teacher knows I am interested, but not so close that others label me a suck-up.

I sit with my back straight.

I look the teacher in the eye so she knows I am listening. I want her to know that at least one student values her effort.

I am ready to answer every question she asks, but I raise my hand tentatively, so as not to appear overly confident.

I am vigilant; I know that the moment I slump or glance away or am unprepared will be the moment when the teacher proclaims my bad behavior for all to hear.

Yesterday, the teacher said that my class was the worst class she has ever taught.

*

For five successive days, I meet another boy in my backyard at the spot where home base is for Wiffle ball games, and we fight until we run out of energy. After the first day, I do not recall why we are fighting, but I enjoy clenching my muscles and meeting an equal force as I try to wrestle him to the ground. After each day's fight, my arms and legs feel heavy and relaxed.

*

How to walk with Steve:

Stay in front of him or behind him; he will not walk beside another person. The advantage of walking in front of him is the ability to set the course. In general, he will follow. Glance back every few seconds because Steve will dart away to see a sign or to veer far away from another approaching person.

I keep a hand outstretched at all times to grab him if he starts running. But I don't touch him unless I sense he is about to run because unexpected touch makes him shout.

*

We have moved into a new house inside the city limits. We moved because my parents discovered that if we are in the city, we can petition the city school district to create an educational program for Steve.

Steve draws a freehand blueprint of the new house. The drawing indicates the correct proportion of all the rooms, which way each door swings, the shape of the toilets, and the fact that there are two basins in the kitchen sink.

In the afternoons, I see Steve standing with his bike on a corner several blocks from our house. He is watching the traffic.

In the evenings, he draws two-dimensional side views of school buses. Each indicates a slightly different number and shape of windows, different words on the sides, and different numbers in the lower right corner.

Steve's lines and letters are shaky, like those of a child younger than he is, but also elegant and careful.

He cuts out the buses and keeps them in a plastic box. One day, I count the bus pictures. There are fifty-two.

*

I ask my mother how she decides what to paint. She takes a ketchup bottle resting on the table in front of us, turns the bottle upside down, puts it back on the table, and gestures toward it. To me, this is brilliant. I understand. My dad has told me that my mom is a great teacher, and now I know it is true.

*

In school, we are asked to bring in a food that the other kids will try blindfolded and guess its identity. I ask my mom what I should bring. She opens the cupboard and takes out a cube of bouillon. "No one will be able to guess this," she says.

In class, one student after another is blindfolded at the front of the room. The teacher puts a piece of apple or a piece of bread or a piece of cheese in each student's mouth, and the student, while still chewing, says the name of the food. When the teacher picks up the bouillon cube, I am confident that my mother was right—no one could guess this. A girl with wavy brown hair approaches, and the teacher puts a white cotton blindfold over her eyes. The teacher removes the shiny blue wrapper, revealing a tiny, grainy brown cube. The girl opens her mouth, and the teacher puts the cube in. The girl throws her hand over her mouth, begins spitting into it, and runs from the room. I have made a terrible mistake.

*

Tomorrow is my tenth birthday. Mom tells me that she remembers when, shortly after my birth, she, my dad, and I were at a park. The air was crisp and the leaves were beautiful and it was the happiest time of her life. The worst time of her life, she says, is when Steve was born and his twin died. I recognize that I have a great duty.

*

I might disturb Mom while she is painting or while she is in her office, and she would look at me with the expression that told me I was breaking her. I might puncture Steve's attention to drawing, and he might begin running and shouting.

As I move through the house, I walk on the balls of my feet so that my heels don't thump on the floor. I step lightly to avoid making the floor creak. When opening a door, I turn the knob all the way, and then slowly pull or push. If the door sticks, I guide it slowly so it makes as little noise as possible. When closing a door, I repeat this process in reverse.

*

Mom is talking about a sculpture created by a family friend, a thin, dark-haired woman who, I recall, visited our house once or twice. The sculpture is in a plaza at my dad's university, in a wide space of land circled by the music building, a dormitory, and the bookstore. My mother says that if the sculpture were small or huge, it might work, but as it is, medium sized, it isn't much of anything. I feel bad for the sculptor, that she has made this mistake.

*

The Case of the Double Kidnapping is the third book in the *Power Boys* series. The cover illustration is dramatic black ink on dark green. The Power Boys—Jack, seventeen, and Chip, fifteen—are in New York City with their father, a famous photographer who takes the boys with him when he travels on assignment. The boys do not have a mother. A drawing opposite the first page shows the boys and their father entering their New York apartment: The boys are smiling and looking expectant; their trousers are perfectly creased. In the scene, the boys joke with one another, causing their father to quiet them. Still, they are good boys. Their father gives them cash and then leaves them for a business appointment. New York City on their own!

In bed, close to lights-out time, I have reached a point in the book where Chip, the blond younger brother, escapes from kidnappers. He is somewhere far outside of the city. He runs for a few blocks, then slows, exhausted, and eventually knocks on the door of a small home. The door is opened by an older woman. At first, she is taken aback by the boy's disheveled appearance and begins to close the door. But something about the earnestness of his expression stops her. He begins to tell his story. The tale is outlandish, but she trusts him. She invites him inside, invites him to sit, to have milk and sandwiches. But, Chip says, we need to call the police. No, the woman says, first you need to eat, then you need to rest.

*

The teacher wheels a film projector into the classroom. She begins to thread the movie, but struggles. I have seen my dad thread movie projectors several times and say, "I'll help. I can do it." As I am saying that, another boy is also volunteering. The teacher, a woman with gray hair and an abrupt manner that usually intimidates me, tells us to go ahead.

I try to thread the apparatus the way I have seen Dad do it, but I soon realize that I am lost in the mechanics of the projector. The other boy points and makes suggestions. We turn on the projector, but the film pools on the floor.

The teacher says, addressing the rest of the class, "Which one of them do you think is most conceited?"

I have a measurement system for moments like these. It is a system for measuring the degree of damage when I have done something horrible, when my face feels as if it is boiling and when my skull feels like it is melting, and when I know I have been recognized as the bad person that I am.

The measurement system is founded on the assumption that each of these incidents is permanent. The incident is on a list. Perhaps if I am perfect from now on, I think, nothing will be added to the list. Yet even if I somehow manage to not add things to the list, nothing can be removed from it.

My unit of measurement is the amount of time that will pass until I do not wake up in the morning with the feeling of my face boiling and my skull melting, accompanied by a memory of the incident.

My goal is not that the sensation or the memory will go away. I know it will not. Only that it retreats to a frequency that will allow me some level of relief until the next incident occurs.

As the word "conceited" throbs through me, I launch my measurement system. I calculate how many days I will have this feeling. That is only way I can keep from screaming.

This incident, I think, will be a seven-week incident. I can hold on for seven weeks.

*

It is morning. My dad is sitting on the edge of his bed. His feet are bare. He wipes his right palm across the sole of his left foot and his left palm across the sole of his right foot. Then he puts on his socks. I imagine that he has wiped his feet this way before putting on his socks since being a child. I feel that I have been with him always, as he does this perfect thing.

*

Our house is full of people and voices. Earlier, we watched the people who are now in our house dance on the basketball court of the university where my dad teaches. We sat close to the court. The dancers seemed tilted all the time. Each dancer somehow swooped in different directions at the same time. It was like the pictures on the West Side Story album, only more like a dream. Sometimes the dancers leaned on one another, pressing their bodies fully together. I wondered if touching each other made them uncomfortable. I also knew that touching each other was a good and not-uncomfortable thing for these people. To the side was a table where two men made the sounds that accompanied the dancers. Faint, lonely piano music with grinding noises on top. Silence. Sometimes words. Whirling sounds. Sounds that I had never heard before but that felt natural and available to anyone who cared to grasp them. Sounds that I thought I, too, could find and hold up as something important to be heard.

After the performance, my dad explained to me that normally these people would not come to Peoria, but that he had written them a letter to see if they would stop here between Chicago and St. Louis, and they had said yes.

Now they are in our house. My mom is upstairs painting. I am listening in case Steve gets out of bed.

The people in our house are liquid, relaxed. I do not understand how they are not nervous when in an unfamiliar house. Somehow, now, the house is their house, and I am excited to be in their house. My dad appears and takes my hand. We move to the center of the room, where two people are sitting cross-legged on the floor playing chess on a small end-table with a smoky glass top. My dad introduces me to the man who made the sound for the dance. His name is John Cage. The man rolls onto his back so he can look up at me. Still on his back, he reaches out a hand to shake mine. He has a wavy smile that seems to come from his belly. He seems more delighted to meet me than anyone ever has been.

He rolls back up into a sitting position and asks if I want to play chess with him.

*

I get a chemistry set. I am a little overwhelmed by the powders and equipment and instructions. I find a simple experiment that involves combining two white powders in water to create a red liquid.

That evening, I am watching TV and my dad appears in the living room. He is holding a white plastic cup like the one I used for the experiment. "This cup was in mom's bathroom. Did you use it for anything?"

"Maybe it's the one I used for my experiment." We have several of these cups, and I have no memory of where I put the cup I used.

"Experiment?"

I remind Dad about the new chemistry set.

"Well, your mom is very sick." I realize that I can hear her now, upstairs, down the hall, faintly, vomiting. I imagine her face as she rises from the toilet, pale, hurt, but not surprised.

I am silent.

"I think you poisoned your mom." He pauses. "Well, yes, I guess that's the word. Poisoned."

I consider this as a sentence: "I poisoned my mother." Yes, I suppose that I have. I assume that, although I don't remember putting the cup in her bathroom, I did it purposefully, the intended target my mom.

Upstairs, I see mom in the doorway to my parents' bedroom, her face looking exactly as I had imagined. She seems not to recognize me.

*

My parents take me to see the new movie Easy Rider three times. Each time at the end, I feel my chest tighten painfully at the first shot and the bright-red blood and the abruptness and finality of death, followed by the hope that the other rider will be spared, followed by another shot and more bright-red blood and an even stronger sense of finality for anyone who is not like others. I like the movies my parents take me to see—*Bonnie and Clyde, Butch Cassidy and the Sundance Kid, Cool Hand Luke*—although all of these people die.

*

I am watching Steve. Mom and Dad and Paul are not at home and will not be home for hours. Steve is sitting on the floor watching *Sesame Street* on our black-and-white television.

I am behind him on the couch.

Steve begins to make the sharp "eyh" sound that he makes when upset.

He says, "I want to watch color TV."

I tell Steve that I'm sorry, but we have a black-and-white TV.

The "eyh" sound, louder. "I want to watch *Sesame Street* on color TV."

"We only have a black-and-white TV."

The "eyh" sound sharper and louder. "I want to watch color TV"—louder and faster.

I suggest we have a snack.

He is up, darting jerkily back and forth in the living room. "I-want-to-watch-color-TV" is now one shouted word.

I try to touch his arm. The "eyh" sound is almost a scream. He jerks away.

"Sit with me. We'll watch *Sesame Street*."

He runs to the front door, opens it, and is gone.

I run out and after him. He is on the sidewalk, dancing back and forth. I approach. He darts toward the neighbors' house, onto the porch. He is looking through a window, I assume looking for their television.

"Steve, they're not home." He pauses. I run onto the porch. He eludes me and is again on the sidewalk. I approach, and he begins running away. I recall how one of his teachers described him as running like a gazelle. The teacher said it as though she didn't like Steve.

I call, "Steve." He pauses, then resumes running. He darts onto the porch of another house. I consider the reaction if I were to ring the doorbell of this neighbor, any neighbor—all strangers to our family—and ask if my little brother can watch *Sesame Street* on their color TV.

I call, "Steve." He looks at me. "We can watch color TV." It is the only thing I can say that will stop him. "We can watch *Sesame Street* on color TV. Come with me."

At our house, I tell Steve to wait, and I go upstairs. I look in the box on the top of dad's dresser, the one with tie clasps and buttons. I dig around, using my fingernails to pick up every piece of loose change I can find.

I tell Steve to come with me. We walk down the long block to Main Street. There we cross the street and wait. Eventually, a bus comes. I put in enough change for Steve's fare and mine. I am not sure I have enough to get us home. I guide him toward a seat. We ride until we reach the farthest street downtown. We get off. Steve and I walk. The sun is intense. We reach Sears. Inside, we walk along an aisle of clothing and jewelry to an escalator. I try to see beyond the second-floor railing. I see something shiny. I guide Steve toward the escalator and up. When we reach the second floor, I see a row of large televisions on stands. We approach them. They are turned on, broadcasting in bright color, each TV a slightly different hue. They all are showing the same show—not *Sesame Street*.

"Color TV," I say to Steve.

"I-want-to-watch-Sesame-Street-on-color-TV."

I glance around. No salespeople are watching. I reach for a dial. There are four channels in Peoria. The channel with *Sesame Street* is channel forty-seven. I turn the knob slowly. It glides through channel twenty-five and through channel thirty-one and then to channel forty-seven. The reception is snowy. I can barely see the picture. The sound is only static. I attempt subtle adjustments but see no improvement.

I look up and notice that I have been seen. A salesman starts toward me, a look of concern on his face. I guide Steve toward the escalator. He allows me to do that.

*

My dad's studio in this house is in the basement. He no longer makes kinetic art. Now he makes movies. Long strips of wood are nailed across the wall. The pointy ends of nails extend at regular intervals, with a break for the editing station. Strips of film hang from the nails. Dad shows me how everything works—he turns a crank that draws film through the viewer. At a certain point, he stops, removes the strip, and cuts it in a device that looks like a miniature guillotine. Then he glues the end of that strip to the end of a strip he removes from a nail. Then he glues the end of that strip to the end of the strip he had spliced to make the film whole again. He shows me the result: A shot panning slowly across a lakeshore, then a cut to a shot of a bicycle riding in the distance, moving from right to left. The combination of these two moving images, putting them together in exactly this way and at exactly this moment, seems both completely arbitrary and completely inevitable. It is quiet and magic.

*

Saturday. The phone rings. My dad answers, listens, says a few words, and hangs up. He goes upstairs to where my mom is painting, comes back down and tells me that my brother Paul was caught shoplifting at a store downtown. Dad is going to pick him up. My legs tremble. As Dad leaves, I turn and see Mom on the stairs. Her arms are stiff at her sides. She seems to sink rather than walk down the stairs. She approaches and faces me.

"Did you know about this?" These words sound like one word and feel like a spear entering my chest.

"No." I did know that Paul had planned to meet a friend at a store and shoplift. He had made a list of things he wanted to shoplift. But I didn't want to get Paul into any further trouble.

Louder. "Did you know about this?"

"No."

"He is at the store. He's being held there." Her enunciation is now like twigs breaking. "What would your grandfather say?"

I am silent.

"Have you ever shoplifted?"

"Yes."

She flinches. "Go to your room." The feeling of falling is so strong it seems impossible to move up the stairs.

Later, we are at the dining room table. Mom is staring into the distance. Her plate is empty. I say, "Mom?" She looks toward me, her face seeming a blur. I say, "Can I get you something to eat?"

"Yes." She gestures toward Paul. "Get me a two-inch-square piece of his skin."

After dinner, after mom has gone upstairs, Dad says to Paul and me that Mom told him this is the worst thing to happen to her since Steve's twin died.

Upstairs that night, I try to calculate how long the falling feeling will last. First, I think two weeks. Then I think two months. Then I accept it: forever. Forever for Paul, and forever for me.

1972-1975

In preparation for a visit from my mother's father, we buy food that he will like, and we buy ingredients for his evening martinis. I wonder about this—the idea that a host would buy things that a visitor would like, rather than a visitor accepting what a host would normally have.

When my grandfather arrives, my mother is girlish, calls him Daddy, waits on him.

At dinner, Grandpa sits at the head of the table, where my dad would normally sit. This seems wrong, seems to diminish my dad in some way.

We begin the meal with salad and rolls. Usually, we serve salad at the same time as the rest of our meal, and we never have rolls. Grandpa puts a pat of butter on his bread plate. He turns to me and says, "Here is how you eat bread." He tears off a small piece of the roll. He butters the small piece. He puts it in his mouth. He swallows, then takes a bite of salad. Then he talks about something I do not understand. Another piece of roll, butter, salad, and talk. He is on his third tiny piece of roll in the amount of time it would normally take me to finish an entire meal. I construct a facial expression meant to depict helplessness, but I cannot catch my mom's or my dad's eyes.

Around noon the next day, I am playing basketball in our next-door neighbor's driveway. I come inside through the kitchen door and see my grandfather sitting alone at the head of the dining room table.

I say, "I'm hungry. I'm going to get myself something to eat."

He says, "I will have two scrambled eggs, toast, and orange juice."

I've never made scrambled eggs before, but I've seen my dad do it. I get out the eggs and a pan, and I do the best I can. When I'm finished, I serve the plate and a glass of orange juice to Grandpa.

That afternoon, Grandpa is having a martini and eating cheese and crackers from the coffee table in our living room. The family is seated around him, including Steve, whom I watch closely, my arm ready to reach out and gather him in if he starts to make his lurching motions or to run away. I know that Mom is concerned that Steve will disturb her father.

Grandpa turns to Steve and says, "Steven, do you like cheese?"

Steve says, "I don't like cheese."

Grandpa says, "I don't know if life would be worth living without cheese."

I wonder what it would be like to love cheese more than anything else.

*

Mom tells me that her mom forced her to be left-handed. She shows me that she can write as well with either hand. She says that her mom forced her to be left-handed so that she would be special.

Mom tells me that her mother talked with her like a friend,

like a conspirator, that they hid things from Mom's father, like her mother's smoking.

I picture Mom and her mother in the park, in fall, on the edge of a patch of woods, leaves on the ground all around them. The sky is overcast. Mom's mother is leaning toward Mom, whispering things to her and perhaps giggling just a bit, although Mom does not laugh.

*

Dad's bare torso is wrapped in a kid's orange life vest. His body's wiry black hair shows in the gaps. The life vest is not very tight, and I can trace the contours of his torso as the vest shifts. He is thinner than I imagined. He is short, but more than that, he looks short. He is the same height as Mom, but she looks long and lean. He looks stocky. So I am surprised to see how thin, almost frail, he looks.

At Lake of the Ozarks, on vacation, we have met a family. We have a rowboat with an outboard motor, but they have a motorboat. The man is tall and commanding. The woman has dimples. They invite us to waterski.

They give me four tries, but I can't get upright; my legs are too scrawny, too weak. Paul gets up for a minute or two and then falls. Mom, wearing a lifebelt rather than a vest the kids wear, looking confident and grim, draws herself up easily and skis for what seems like a long time. As she skis, my dad says to me, "Your mom is a natural athlete." I have never seen her play any sport. I wonder if she used to play sports but stopped when she married Dad, or when she came to Peoria, or when the kids were born.

Next, the man hands Dad the lifebelt, but Dad gestures for the full life vest.

In the water, as the boat gathers speed, Dad emerges, holding the line, wobbly, but upright, and he stays that way as the boat gains speed.

He looks nowhere near as athletic as Mom. He looks nothing like any athlete I have ever seen on television. He is dark, hairy, short, thin, but not muscular. I picture him next to the other teachers in the art department, his movements looking mechanical next to those of his colleagues—who seemed graceful, overflowing with wit and confidence.

And Dad has never waterskied in his life, although his wife skied like a pro her first time.

Although his legs wobble, he stays upright. His short, hairy arms remain taut and his hands grip the handle, his body has a kind of sturdiness underneath the child's life vest.

To me, he looks beautiful.

*

In school, the first day after summer vacation, I ask a girl if she wants to be my girlfriend. While asking, I lean on the water fountain handle and spray water onto my shirt. She says yes. But after the incident with the water fountain, I doubt I will have the courage to speak to her again.

*

My dad is busy, and so my mom takes me to my allergist appointment. She pulls the car up to the front door of the clinic and I get out. After the appointment, I wait outside the clinic for Mom to pick me up.

A good amount of time passes, and Mom has not arrived.

I go back into the clinic and use the bathroom. After washing my hands, I take a black plastic comb from my back pocket. My hair is parted on the side in the traditional manner, my ears partially covered. I drag the edge of my comb down the center of my scalp and part my hair in the middle, like the pop star David Cassidy's hair.

My new hair style feels bold. I feel as though I am beginning to understand my true self, a self that is confident, perhaps even flamboyant, maybe a bit rebellious, and certainly far beyond the confines of Peoria.

As I wait outside the clinic in my bold new hair style, I open the door for each person who approaches. I want these people to know that even a counterculture person like myself can be polite.

My mom arrives and, when I climb into the car, she makes no comment about my hair. Nor does anyone mention my hair at home. At the dining room table that evening, after we have taken our first few bites of dinner, my mom says to the table at large, "Well, what do we think of Rob's new hair style?"

I look around and see no reaction from my father or Paul. Steve is repeatedly touching his knife handle with his index finger. I look at my mom. She shakes her head. After dinner, I comb my hair back to the way it has been.

*

I am talking to Mom upstairs in her office. She walks toward the bathroom and motions me to follow. She sits to pee, I sit on a window ledge, and we continue our conversation. I hear voices below. I look down out the window and see three neighborhood kids—two girls and one boy—in our back yard. I rarely see the neighborhood kids, and they are never in our yard.

They see me in the window and call up to me.

I wave, and they call again.

My mom asks, "What is that?"

"Kids outside."

My mom wipes, pulls up her pants, and hurries from the room. I follow her. She walks quickly down the steps. In the kitchen, she flings open the back door and walks outside. I wait at the door. I can see Mom's profile and the kids' faces.

Mom is shouting. "I was sitting on the toilet having a conversation with my son when you started yelling. That was very rude."

From the doorway, I see the confused expressions of the kids, who look at each other and move away.

*

My mother has told me several times that she stopped painting for ten years after my little brother's twin died. Now I walk around the house, studying the dates on her paintings. Each has her full name and the last two digits of the year. I see no break in the chronology.

*

We drive from Peoria to the West Coast.

In San Francisco, we meet Dad's best friend from boyhood—and his friend's wife and daughter. His grown son is traveling in South America. Something about the family feels thick. There is a thickness of history, individually and as a family; of each one's complete comfort and confidence; of each one's ability to penetrate, to see underneath his or her surroundings. Dad's friend is a writer with several books published, one about the riots at San Francisco State University in 1968. I picture Dad's friend walking through the riots, seeing them deeply, witnessing them. Dad tells me that his friend is sick—he had cancer, and the treatment fixed the cancer but damaged his heart. I am told that he is weak, has trouble climbing the stairs in his house, but to me he looks strong. The top two buttons of his shirt are unbuttoned. He is tan. Dad tells me that his friend was the starting quarterback on the Brooklyn College football team and had offers from the pros but chose to be a writer. I can easily imagine Dad's friend, even now, grabbing a football and making a long downfield pass.

Dad's friend is telling a story about his son. In the South American country where his son is currently traveling with friends, the son was caught shoplifting. "You know, Jerry," Dad's friend says, "like we used to do when we were kids. They threw him in jail. What the hell?"

I glance at my mom, whose lips are pursed. I feel as though Dad's friend has extended an arm to separate me ever so slightly from my mother.

The grown-ups go out one evening, and I watch Steve. I am worried about what the family's daughter will think of Steve. When she serves us food, he starts to get up from the table, but I am able to ease him back into his chair. After dinner, we watch a comedy program on television. Whenever the laugh track of the show comes on, Steve puts his shoulders up toward his ears and makes a grunting growl, which is his new sound. His sound gets louder each time the laugh track plays. I don't know whether Steve has had a pill today. My parents don't want Steve to take pills and plan to stop them as soon as we return from this trip, but I find the pill bottle and give him one. Soon he quiets down, and we settle back to watch the TV show.

We drive from San Francisco to the interior of Washington State to what looks like an abandoned resort. There, my mother's mother is living with a man who runs the resort. We are told it is "off season," but the weather is nice, and if people aren't here now, I don't know when they would be.

My mother's mother is in a wheelchair. She darts around the tiny kitchen, where we congregate in the tiny house. Her face looks at once tense and blank. She orders the man to get us things. He is thin and responds quickly.

When the man finds out that my bother Paul and I are interested in music, he tells us that he used to play in swing bands and that one band used a song he wrote as its theme song.

"They don't want to hear about that," my grandmother says.

The next day, we swim in the resort's small pool. We boys

splash around in the shallow end, which is not very far from the deep end, where my mom and dad take turns diving, my mom smoothly and my dad competently but awkwardly.

After a dive, my dad comes to the surface making lurching motions with his arms. My mom and the man pull him toward the side of the pool. He is making a noise that is not quite gasping, but attempting to gasp. They pull him up and lay him on the ground. I look for Steve. My dad is trying to breathe. My mom tells us to go into the house. I watch out the window as the man pulls a car up near the pool.

"It would take too long to wait for an ambulance in this godforsaken place," my grandmother says. She sounds to me more concerned about insulting the place this man has taken her to live than trying to save my father.

My brothers and I spend the evening with our grandmother, who tells us stories of friends and family of hers who had sudden illnesses or injury. In her stories, all of the people die.

Two days later, we visit Dad in a tiny hospital. There is something wrong with his epiglottis, Mom tells us. He looks tiny and pale in the bed.

A few days later, we pack. Mom will drive us to the hospital. We will pick up Dad and start our drive home. I carry bags to the car. Outside, the man who lives with my grandmother waves me toward him and around the side of the house. He sings me the song he wrote that the swing band used as its theme.

*

Steve loses the plastic box holding his one hundred or more drawings of different school buses. Steve says, "I lost my buses."

51

He says this again and again. He darts around the house. He makes his growl-groan sound. The sound shifts into a wail. He shouts. He shouts, "I lost my buses. I will never have them again." He says this all day for one day, two days, three days. Finally, my dad finds the box. He makes a fire in our fireplace and burns the drawings. "I don't ever want us to have to go through this again," he says. Steve watches, screaming.

*

Until this year, at recess I used to play basketball with the boys and everyone liked me and I liked everyone. This year, I just want to walk on the playground and talk to my friend Dena, the second shortest girl in class, about the book *A Clockwork Orange*, about David Bowie, about Andy Warhol.

I like that I like these things. I like talking with Dena about them. I am proud of myself. I am bursting with excitement about these things.

At the same time, the kids I used to play with and who used to like me now don't like me. No, it's not that they don't like me, or that they have forgotten that I exist, but that they are in the process of closing ranks into a new kind of group—a group I suspect has a language, a set of concerns, a way of interacting that I will never understand, and that this group looks and behaves like most of the people I see around town, and that I will forever be excluded from this group. I am mourning this change.

After school, I go upstairs to my room and lie face-down on my bed and cry. I have been doing this for four days.

I hear the door open and, still crying, I turn and see my dad.

"I see you've been upset for a few days," he says.

I don't respond.

"Your mom and I are concerned. We wonder if you need to see someone."

I turn away and cry harder. This is the last day I go up to my room and cry.

*

We drive through a town called DuBois. My mom says the name using the French pronunciation.

My dad says, "Actually, the people who live here pronounce it 'Du-Boyz.'"

My mom says, "The proper pronunciation is the French," and she repeats that pronunciation.

My dad says, "I think the people who live there should be able to say how the town's name is pronounced."

My mom says, "The proper pronunciation is the French."

*

Through the front window, I watch my piano teacher approach our house. He smiles as he walks. He walks briskly. But the defining characteristic of his walk is its stiffness. He walks like a marching soldier, a happy soldier, a solder in a hurry, a soldier who swings his arms crisply because he likes swinging his arms crisply. My teacher thinks of me as a special student. A student he has had for a long time. A student who plays well (or at least better than most of his other students). A student who practices (or at least more than most of his other students). A student who will play at recitals (I fear them but like the accolades). My piano teacher also teaches voice, and at his request, I joined a church choir he led (although I spent a fair amount of time mouthing the words, and once, outside the church, which was on a hill, my dad didn't fully set his parking brake, and the car rolled backwards down the hill and hit another car).

I feel no connection to the music I am taught, and I don't sight-read well, and I cannot simply sit and play without first slowly learning the music. I have wanted to quit for several years. But of course, I can't. I couldn't bear disappointing my teacher, smiling and marching up the walk.

Once, my piano teacher stopped by my house briefly with his younger brother. His brother could not sit still, held his hands in an awkward way, turned his head back and forth, and spoke in a slurred voice. I looked at my piano teacher, so crisp and upright and smiling and self-possessed sitting next to his brother, and I thought, "Oh, you're one of me." But we did not speak about that.

*

In our house, my dad is heading for the staircase. I am a few steps behind. We are talking about an author. My dad says, his voice teasing, "Well, he's no Raymond Chandler."

Raymond Chandler is my favorite writer. I know that Dad thinks Raymond Chandler is silly, that Dad lumps him in with second-rate writers. My dad, I know in that moment, thinks of me as a child.

My face burns. I grab the handrail at the base of the staircase and pull. It comes out of the wall, bringing with it a shower of plaster pieces and dust. A crack forms halfway up the wall along the course of the stairs, creating a huge scar in the beautifully textured surface of the wall.

*

A music teacher at school—a burly man—asks me to learn a piece to play at a student concert. I say, "I'll do the best I can." To me, this is a sacred oath. I will do not fairly well, but my best. My desire to do my best is sacred.

The teacher, throwing back his shoulders, says, "Oh. I see. You'll just do the best you can. If you asked me to do something, and I said…" here he adopts a whiny voice, "'I'll just do the best I can,' how would you feel? Would you feel confident that I would come through for you? I want people who will come through for me."

I have failed before even starting.

*

With Dad in the university art building, I say, "You can't expect me to behave rationally because I'm not old enough to behave rationally."

Dad smiles and shakes his head. "Sorry, but if you're rational enough to make that argument then you're old enough to behave rationally."

I want to explain that it isn't so simple but can't find the right phrasing.

*

I am in the living room. It is evening. Mom is on the couch, which is unusual. Usually, she spends evenings in her office. I rarely think about what she might do in her office. I only think about it when I go into her office to say something to her, and I see the half-open closet door and the open carton of Schlitz beer cans on the closet floor.

She is telling me that two teachers quit at the Peoria arts center where she oversees education as a part-time job. She says she doesn't know what she is going to do. I suggest that she recruit more teachers from among Dad's art students. She could ask Dad, I say, or she could put a notice up on the bulletin board in the art building. She seems not to hear me. She says, "I don't know what I'm going to do." She says it again, "I don't know what I'm going to do," addressing the words to the wall beside and above me. She stands and starts for the stairs, veering a bit off course. She mounts one step, pauses, then another, her loose pantlegs jiggling. "Can you," she says, pauses, "can you…" The words sound like rubber bands being twisted. She holds the rail, sinks to her knees.

I leave her there and head to the basement, where my dad is editing film.

"Your wife," I say, "is having a problem getting up the stairs." The anger in the words "your wife" feels good.

Upstairs, he grasps Mom's shoulders and tilts her back, but her head lolls to one side. He says, "How many did you take?"

She shakes her head and starts to sink again.

"Did you take two?"

She moves her head, but it is hard to tell if it is a nod or a shake.

Dad grips her shoulders harder. "Did you take more?"

I walk around them and go up to my room.

*

I stand in the main gathering area of the shopping mall, the largest shopping mall in the country.

It is after midnight. On the floor around me are couples on mats, some covered in blankets. Maybe fifty couples, maybe more. All the couples have their lips together. In theory, they are kissing. But at this point, after many hours, it is more accurate to say that they are holding their lips together. Some drink through straws while kissing. One man smokes, careful that the cigarette does not separate his lips from his partner's lips.

My job is to watch for whether any couple's lips separate during the night.

I have been told to be scrupulous because, depending on the outcome, this may go into the Guinness Book of World Records for world's longest kiss.

The day before, I rode from Peoria to Chicago on a bus. It was dark when I got to Chicago. I transferred to the train that would take me to the suburb where I had reserved a room at a hotel within walking distance of the mall. I had been a little surprised that it was possible for a thirteen-year-old to call a hotel and make a reservation.

On the train, the conductor looked at my ticket and told me I was going the wrong way. He consulted his worn print timetable and said "hmm" a few times, while I felt like the train and I were a silk scarf, slipping off the edge of the table. The conductor told me that I should get off at the next stop and take the train going the other direction. He looked concerned as he was saying this. The problem, he said, was that the train going the other way would arrive very soon after we passed the station—so soon that I would not have time to go down the stairs and then up to the other side of the platform. I would need to walk across the tracks and climb up onto the platform. Also, it was the last train of the night.

I followed his instructions. On the other side of the platform, I waited, in the dark, watching for the train's headlights, which I knew may already have passed. I wasn't sure what I would do if I had missed it. I saw nothing but dark past the dim overhead lights of the station. I wanted the train to come, I was worried that it wouldn't, but at the same time I liked the dark pressing in on me from all directions. I pictured myself walking into it and having adventures.

After several hours of watching the couples, a woman relieves me. She is wearing a tight black t-shirt with the word "KISS" in rhinestones across the front. I lie on my side on a wooden-slatted bench nearby and sleep. In the morning, I go through temporary plywood doors into an empty retail space, the floor covered in plastic sheeting, which is the event's headquarters. I take a bagel from the catering table. There are no bagels in Peoria, but I like them when our family visits New York.

Soon, the members of a rock band arrive with some helpers.

They wear garish white makeup with huge black and red and silver shapes on their faces—one looks like a vampire, another has a huge star over his eye. Another looks like a cat. Another looks like a fantasy spaceman. Their hair is long and black and seems to rise from their heads in defiance of gravity. They wear black leather outfits and huge platform shoes, which they have to lift and set down carefully so as not to trip on the plastic sheeting's seams. I take some pictures of them with my dad's camera. The band's name is KISS, and the kissing marathon is a promotion to spread the word about the band, which is not well known outside of New York City. I wrote a letter to the band's management after its first album was released, wanting to let the band and management know that I had enjoyed the record because I assumed few people would buy a record by a band that looked so strange. I wanted them to be encouraged. The management called me a few weeks later and asked if I wanted to help out at this event outside Chicago.

When the band leaves the empty store, a large crowd has formed in the mall. It is Saturday. The crowd steps around the kissing couples and on up the broad stairs that cascade around them. Above, people walk on what looks like multiple catwalks to and from pockets of stores. The band steps through the crowd and through the kissers. Shoppers look at them from the corners of their eyes. The president of the band's record label makes an announcement into a hand-held microphone.

That afternoon, when I meet my parents in our family car, which is pulled up to a curb in the parking lot outside the mall, I am wearing a pair of glittery light-blue pants and a pair of green platform shoes. My mom and dad say that they may not give me money to spend on clothes again if make such impractical purchases.

After I had woken on the bench, one of the organizers told me that during the night, a couple had fallen asleep and had fallen away from each other's lips. When they awoke, they had been notified and left the mall.

As we drive home to Peoria, I imagine the couple folding their mat and blankets, and stepping through the other kissers, heavy with disappointment and shame.

*

Mom clearly enunciates the final letter of each word—most notably Ts and Ds. I have never heard anyone enunciate that way. It's as if she is twisting the end of each word, snapping it off, and tossing it away with some mixture of pride and annoyance.

When I say "hopefully," Mom instructs me that the appropriate phrase is "it is to be hoped."

Usually when Mom corrects my grammar, my response is that she may be right, but nobody talks that way.

She then cites a rule. However, I notice a slight pause before she says something like "object of the preposition" or "subjunctive mood." That slight pause, along with the disconnection between what she is saying and what I remember from school, suggests to me that she is bullshitting.

*

The door across the hall is open. I am in the dormitory at a summer arts institute for high school students. I am not yet a high school student, but the program made an exception for me. The boy across the hall has left his room with a load of laundry. I make sure no one is watching and then enter his room, heading straight for his dresser. I open the top drawer and see a $20 bill. Earlier in the day, I saw him put the money in the drawer. I take the bill and slip back into my room. I stay there, trying to read but not able to see the words. In the evening, from my bed, I can see people milling around the hall and can hear them chatting and talking in silly voices and laughing. I get along well with them—I made friends with them easily. But now I need to stay lying on my bed. The boy across the hall has entered and left his room twice with his laundry basket. Now I hear him telling the others in the hall that he had had $20 in his dresser drawer and now it is gone. I am different from everyone else here because I am the one who stole $20 from a boy. I also know that for the rest of my life I will have a bad feeling when I see this building, which is next to the building where I have my piano lessons. I am beginning to be concerned about the number of places and words that give me this feeling. I can foresee a day when I cannot go anywhere or hear any words or see any movies or listen to any music without this feeling pulling up through my chest and into my throat. I recall an episode of the TV show *Batman* in which Batman and Robin are in a cave. The walls of the cave are closing in. Batman and Robin prop their backs against one wall and put their feet against the opposite wall, but to no avail. As I watched the scene, when I was a small boy, I understood intellectually that Batman and Robin would be fine, that they escaped danger in every episode, that the TV show would have to stop if Batman and Robin were killed. Still, I also knew, as they fought against the walls closing in, that they would die.

*

The garage is full of college students—many art students of my dad's. Loud music is playing. The crowd looks like a photo of a party in one of my dad's art magazines. My dad and I are at the edge of the crowd. The rock music stops, replaced with a loud rendition of "Here Comes the Bride." The crowd stops talking. Two men emerge from the back corners of the garage. One is wearing an American flag as a cape. They remind me of Andy Warhol's stars at The Factory, of Lance Loud and his friend Kristian Hoffman from my favorite TV show, *An American Family*. The two men meet and enter the crowd, which divides to accept them. Once through the crowd, they are met by a man who has shoulder-length hair with gray streaks. The man begins to speak. He talks about the importance of a loving relationship, about the importance of commitment, about the bright future the two have before them. He mentions Richard Nixon. The two men recite wedding vows, similar to ones I have heard on TV shows. The man with gray hair says, "I now pronounce you married," and the two men kiss deeply and with joy, in a way I have never seen so close to me.

*

I am struggling to breathe. Above the water's surface, I hear a belittling voice shouting at me. The gist of the shouts is that I should keep going. It seems entirely realistic that I might die. I reach the end of the pool, pull myself out, and go sit on the floor next to a row of other boys. The PE coach begins excoriating the next swimmer. I have never heard someone shout so loudly, express anger so casually. I am under his control. It is the second day in high school, and I will be under his control for months.

The boy sitting on the floor next to me smacks his knee against my knee rapidly, as though with a nervous twitch. But when I turn toward him he says, as if in a chant, "You're gonna give me your money, you're gonna give me your money, I'm gonna beat the shit out of you, you're gonna give me your money." He is skinny, probably shorter than I am. His eyes look perfectly calm. He continues tattooing my knee. "You're gonna give me your money. You're gonna give me your money. I'm gonna beat the shit out of you."

*

During classes, I write notes of what I will talk about on the phone that evening with my friend Dena, who goes to another high school. Each note feels as though it is small and good—a piece of safety.

*

Some seniors I met the summer before at a photography class suggest I join them on the yearbook staff. They show me how to forge passes to skip classes. I shoot a roll of film, develop it in the darkroom, make some prints. Then I don't shoot anything for a week. I forget how to develop film. I sit in the yearbook office the rest of the year and hope no one notices that I don't take any pictures. The seniors I know come in and out of the lounge, and they acknowledge me, but they are friends with each other, not with me.

One day I am sitting in the lounge. The only other person there is a senior girl at a desk. She says, "This is a funny article."

There is no reason for her talk with me, much less share a magazine article with me. I know immediately she is taking pity on me.

"See," she says, "It's a list of spoilers for famous movies." I stand up and look down at the desk. She reads, "Rosebud is Citizen Kane's sled."

I understand the humor, but I also see a thread of cruelty and smugness. I wonder what the author would think if the article actually ruined a great movie for someone.

*

From the empty shoe store showroom, I look into the mall. Our storefront faces the entrance to the down escalator. The store manager, a bony man with a droopy mustache who moves like a marionette, stands next to me, smoking a cigarette. A heavyset woman is poised at the top of the escalator, accompanied by a young girl. The woman is in mid-step, her right foot hovering over the retreating escalator steps. She pulls her foot back, then extends it again, this time lightly touching the moving steps before she pulls it back. The girl says, "It's OK Mom. Go ahead. You can do it. You won't fall."

Laughter is leaking out of the store manager, his mustache twitching. He butts his cigarette, covers his mouth, and turns away.

I turn toward a rack of women's dress shoes. Putting one foot on a moving stair, I think, is indeed a significant act of trust.

I lied about my age to get this job, saying I was 16 when I am only 14. Most days I fear being discovered. My first job was as a bus boy at a pizza restaurant. Soon I was promoted to making pizza. The first night I made pizza, I forgot to put spices on a pizza. That evening, I thought about the people who ordered a pizza, looking forward to a happy dinner and a good-tasting pizza, who got a pizza with no spices. Even now at the shoe store, I still think about those people and their disappointment.

My favorite part about the job is running stock. I love that phrase, "running stock." It feels animated, forceful. We would get a new shipment of shoes and stack the boxes in the back room next to the spot where the shoes belong, based on their stock numbers.

I also love the stock numbers. A two-digit code indicates whether the shoe is for men, women, or children. A four-digit code indicates the type of shoe: dress, casual, athletic, and so forth. Finally, a six-digit code is a unique number for the style.

The sense of order, of clean organization, from these codes is intoxicating.

Here is how to run stock: I count the number of boxes on the floor. Then I count the number of gaps in the stock—holes where boxes could be—moving back from the place where the new stock should be. Then I move the shoe boxes to fill each gap. The gap gets larger and larger until it will fit the new shipment, which I then put onto the shelves.

No people. No uncertainty. A simple process with specific results.

I don't mind selling shoes. Rather, I don't mind showing people shoes. I hold back when they are trying to make a decision about buying the shoes. Once I said to a customer, "It's all right, you don't have to get them, just think about it." She bought the shoes but looked at me in a hurt way, as though by saying that, I had coerced her into buying them. Later, as I walked in the mall to get lunch, I saw the woman, she saw me, and she turned away quickly with a look of fear and shame. After that, I would just be quiet, and people either bought the shoes or didn't.

As the salespeople go in and out of the back room, we take puffs of cigarettes. Sometimes, in the evening, there is a bottle of whiskey, which we sip from between customers or when going to get a pair of shoes for a customer.

*

My dad and I confer, and we decide the best school for me to attend for my second year in high school is a Catholic school. I will not have to go to religious ceremonies, just take a history of religion class.

The school is brighter, cleaner than the previous one. The first day of school, in the spacious common area, students who know each other—presumably from the previous year and from Catholic elementary school groups—chat or, as my dad would say, horse around. The girls wear knee-length checked skirts, white knee socks, and white blouses. The boys wear dark slacks, white shirts, and ties that, already, first thing in the day, are loosened and askew.

A boy approaches me. He is about my age, but more filled out, taller, more handsome. He stands directly facing me, close to me. His hair is combed and in place. His tie is loosened just a bit and hanging straight. His shirt is barely wrinkled.

"You stupid son of a bitch," he says in a clear voice with good enunciation. "I don't want you anywhere near me. I don't want to see your face."

I would think he is talking to someone beside or behind me, but his eyes are fixed directly to mine.

He walks away. I sit, take a notebook from my backpack, and write random words. Through the buzzing in my head, something clicks.

A few weeks ago, my mom confronted me in our living room: "I wish you wouldn't smoke."

"What?"

"Mrs. Barnes saw you smoking beside her van."

This was simply untrue. I didn't do it. But I suspected I knew who had.

"Mom, I really and truly did not do that. I wish you wouldn't just assume the worst. I am sure it was Billy. You know, Billy— the Robinson's kid. He looks just like me. He lives just down the street. It's just the kind of thing he would do."

My mom didn't believe me.

Now I remember that Billy's mom found out I was going to the Catholic high school and wanted to sell us Billy's school jacket because he was switching schools. This morning's accosting is a case of mistaken identity.

But I still feel raw all day, and I keep writing nonsense in my notebook when I'm not listening to teachers.

The next day, the same boy approaches me.

"Hey, man," he says. "I'm really sorry. I thought you were someone else."

After school, I tell my mom what happened. "See?" I said. "It's the same thing with the kid smoking by the van. It was the other kid, not me."

She shrugs and walks away.

*

I like my English teacher. He looks like Dustin Hoffman playing Carl Bernstein in *All the President's Men*. Short, hair over the collar, a little stocky, a sense of energy in his walk. We read good books in his class, and I don't get static from the other kids when I raise my hand and offer an interpretation.

Today, we are going through a vocabulary exercise in class. It is nothing, a breeze. Each student has to pronounce a word that was presumed to be a new one for us. When I get to my word—a word I know—I mispronounce it.

I know I am the best student in the class. More importantly, I know that the teacher knows I am the student who cares the most in class, that I think hard about the reading and am excited to contribute and have something approaching real insight. If there were brownie points for my performance, I would have them piled to the roof.

But I have mispronounced a word that I know.

"Sorry," I say.

He looks puzzled. "That's okay."

I do a quick calculation. How long will I feel the mortification of mispronouncing the word and perplexing the teacher? I figure it will fade after three weeks.

*

I return home from work at the shoe store, say hi to my mom in her bedroom, where she is folding laundry, and ask, "Do you want to hear something insulting?"

She frowns. "I don't know, do I?"

I know I have made a terrible mistake. I just wanted to make conversation. Now I can't think of any way to extricate myself. I go on, feeling doomed.

"The cashier asked me if that was my grandmother with me in the store shopping this weekend."

The dimension of my misstep is immediately apparent. My mom's face loses all shape. She sits on the edge of the bed.

"I'm sorry," I say, "I'm sorry. I didn't, I didn't mean." My chest is pounding My lips are hot. "I'm sorry."

My thought was that the cashier's observation was absurd. My mom does not look like a grandmother. Without examining the likelihood of my mom's reaction, I assumed she would see the absurdity. But of course, she doesn't. No one would. No one would take the comment as anything other than a damning insult.

I lie face-down on my bed. Later, before dinner, my dad knocks, enters, and sits on my bed. I turn my head toward him but keep it on the pillow.

"Your mom is pretty upset," he says.

"I know." The words feel like a moan.

"I think your mom looks very good," he says.

"She does," I say. I don't have the energy to explain that I, too, think the comment is absurd. I note that Dad has the presence of mind to omit the phrase "for her age," even when talking to me. I vow to learn from his tact.

He says, "You can't say to someone, 'Do you want to hear something insulting?' and expect the person to say no."

I put my face into my pillow. This mistake may fade, but only to the minute degree that I will be able to repress it just enough to continue to exist.

When I enter the dining room, Mom looks at me and says, "Do you want to hear something insulting?"

*

The teacher wears a large paper clip on his collar and has a goofy smile and floppy limbs. It is the summer after my sophomore year in high school, and I am taking a class on the Midwest in American literature at the university where my dad teaches. My favorite book is *Winesburg, Ohio* by Sherwood Anderson. I love the way the teacher voices lines from the main character's mother. In the book, the mother seems to me to be demented, embarrassing, and sad. But in the teacher's voice, she seems mad in a way that is fun, perhaps admirable, perhaps even necessary.

A few weeks later, I receive an envelope in the mail from the university. It contains an enrollment form for the fall term. One sheet, two-sided.

My parents are in Europe for a month, their first trip overseas, an unheard-of luxury to celebrate my dad's fiftieth birthday. I find it hard to imagine my father and mother together alone for so long. What do they talk about? One of Dad's students is helping watch Steve and driving us places.

I call the university admissions office. I ask whether, because the university sent me an enrollment form, I can enroll for the fall semester, even though I am still in high school. The person says, yes, I can enroll part-time for the first semester and then the university would consider accepting me full-time for the spring semester.

I know that my elementary-school principal now works for the city school district. I look up the number, and ask him whether I can leave high school at age fifteen without graduating if I am going to college. He checks with the school district's attorney, calls me back, and says that's fine.

When my parents return, I tell Dad my plans.

*

The lines and letters of Steve's drawings still have the shakiness of a much younger child, but he can draw a freehand map of the entire city of Peoria—all proportions accurate, every street represented. He can also create a blueprint-style drawing of every building he visits. Most wonderful to me are his street signs. They are no mere representation of a sign, with accurate shape, letters, and symbols. Unlike the two-dimensional, diagrammatic nature of his blueprints and maps and bus drawings, his signs subtly capture his perspective of looking up at the signs. More impressive, he captures the fact that few signs are absolutely perpendicular to the ground. Steve's signs stand at a slight angle, which, along with their shaky lines and letters, give them a sense of well-earned nobility.

*

The university is two blocks from our house. That is fine. I can come and go from the university buildings before and after classes. That is a freedom like none I have ever felt, and that is fine. The classes are interesting and the teachers are friendly and know a lot. That is fine.

I spend my time either in class or at home or going to movies with my friend Dena, who is still in high school, or working at the shoe store. That is fine.

I get braces on my teeth. I take twenty tablets of aspirin over the course of several hours, hoping I will show signs of an overdose but not actually kill myself, and my dad will understand the extent of my humiliation and let me have the braces removed.

In my college classes, I see boys and girls—looking impossibly older than I am—holding hands.

On our spring family trip to New York, I get copies of *The Village Voice*.

At home, I study the classified sections.

I tell my Dad that I have a plan.

My mom says to me one morning, "I hear you're leaving us."

I say, "Yes."

*

In the car, Mom has on no makeup and turns her head abruptly from side to side. She tells me that my footsteps upstairs, while I was cleaning and packing, kept her awake all night. We arrive at the bus station. The sun is bright but not yet high in the sky. In Chicago, I will walk from the bus station to the train station. I take my suitcase out of the back of the station wagon, and she gets out of the car, and I say good bye, and she says good bye.

1975-1977

As I walked down the aisle of the dark train car, I saw passengers with their eyes closed, sitting up or on their sides, or murmuring to seat mates. In the lounge car, however, I encountered a pleasant burst of light and sound, and I saw people sitting and standing at the various tables, chatting and laughing, making their way to and from the refreshment counter.

I got a coke. None of the tables were empty, but I guessed that people just congregated randomly. I sat at a table with two middle-aged men.

As I sipped my coke, I watched a mother and daughter across the aisle. I had seen them earlier in the day, sitting in my car. The mother's face seemed to be all circles—round chin, round eyes, round dimples, a curl of hair hanging along each temple, and the most prominent feature: high, round cheeks. Her face looked like a line drawing in one of my parents' European art magazines. She wore bright colors, but the colors were unable to compete for attention with her face.

Her daughter, about ten years old, was dressed in similarly bright colors. However, the colors overwhelmed her face, which was as flat as her mother's was round.

The men across from me were talking about trucking. One of them glanced at me and asked if I wanted some whiskey in my coke. I said yes, and he drew a paper bag from his windbreaker, unscrewed the mouth protruding from the top, and poured some into my cup.

The mother was sitting on the edge of a table fully occupied by men. The mother's smile accentuated the roundness of her face. She spoke loudly and laughed, and all the men laughed too. More men joined the table, the mother became more animated, and the volume grew louder.

The men across from me stopped talking, turned, and watched the woman. The daughter was sitting on the floor nearby, leaning against the side of the car. Every so often she would stand, take a few steps one way and then the other, and sit again.

The mother was crying out over the voices, "Oh, yes I can. You bet I can." She looked around and saw her daughter. She cried out in the same voice she used to the men, "Honey, go get my bag!"

Without looking at her mother, the girl left the car. She returned with a canvas bag that she set on the table before returning to her spot on the floor.

The mother unzipped the bag and withdrew a handful of white cards. She scattered them on the table for the men to see. She started handing out cards to people standing nearby. She dropped stacks of cards on other tables in the vicinity, including mine. I reached for one.

It was a business card, featuring a picture of the woman in clown makeup with a black bowler and with a bright red nose.

To my eye, she barely needed the makeup. Her features melded into those of a clown perfectly. What other profession could she have?

She was now pulling uninflated balloons from the bag.

She stretched the plastic and began blowing them up, expertly twisting and looping and tying them into a poodle, a bunny, a pig, a mouse. The men laughed and laughed, and everyone continued to drink their beer.

The balloons made the rounds, eventually landing on the floor. The girl rose from the floor and approached the table. There, she took a few steps in one direction, and then a few steps in another, stomping on and popping her mother's balloons.

*

An egg was balanced on the stove. In Peoria, we had an electric stove, but I was pleased to discover that here I had a gas stove, like my grandma's in Brooklyn, with a grate that looked like a spider. The stove was filthy, and on one arm of the grate rested this egg, balanced on its tip.

I did not understand how the egg sat there, on its tip, without falling.

I touched the egg with one finger, holding my other hand nearby in case the egg fell. It didn't. I grasped it with two fingers and a thumb and pulled a bit harder. Resistance. I pulled harder still, and the egg broke. The apartment exploded with the smell. I believed I could see bugs flying out of the egg. I opened the window, somehow more satisfied with my home than when I had walked in.

*

I was in a dark Chinese restaurant up a few steps from the sidewalk on MacDougal Street.

I sat at a large round table. I knew one person at the table—a friend of my brother who was attending Columbia. He worked for one of the people at the table. I had been in New York for just a few days.

My overwhelming sense was of simultaneity. They talked simultaneously. They drank from the same wine bottles, pulled one after another from a brown paper bag on the floor next to my friend's boss. The people looked alike—all dressed with a kind of blissful casualness, all with unrestrained hair and big, relaxed laughs and gestures. My friend's boss had a waxed mustache with the thinnest possible upturned ends.

The food appeared and was set on a lazy Susan in the center of the table. I had never eaten Chinese food before. Eating more than one kind of Chinese food seemed overwhelming.

I had no choice. I could not simply refuse to eat. I served myself the concoction that looked the least threatening. I took a small forkful and put half of it in my mouth.

The noise and activity receded to a pleasant buzz in the background. I felt as though my chest were expanding. I felt a fuzziness in my head. I felt as though I were tasting food for the first time.

*

Dust seemed to float in the air. Patches of the floor were sawdust, patches wood. No music played. No one sat at the bar or on the mismatched chairs at the tables scattered across the floor. The tiny stage, just a small step up from the floor, was bare. I asked the bartender, her features hard to discern in the haze, for a club soda. I expected resistance to a sixteen-year-old in the bar, but she made no comment. Taking my glass, I walked the perimeter of the main room, then wound through the tables and chairs, trying to appear as though I either had a purpose or did not need one.

I followed a clacking sound and came to a doorway. The room beyond was darker than the main room and barely large enough for the scarred pool table it contained. One man, his skin, knit cap, and clothes the same gray as the air, carried his cue loosely in one hand as he circled the table. Another man leaned in a corner, his cue leaning beside him.

The shooter took his shot, missed, and traded places with the other man.

When the first shooter again approached the table, he glanced at me and gestured with his left hand, a small but sweeping gesture.

He said, "If you want to give the world an enema, put the nozzle right here."

Later, people arrived at the club, which was called CBGB, and musicians played, musicians I had read about in magazines. I went looking for the pool players, but they were gone.

*

The man with the handlebar mustache and his wife invited me to a Western-themed bar on the Upper East Side, where upstairs a musical comedy based on a Bret Harte story was being performed. It took place in a mining town and featured a strong-willed schoolmaster's daughter, a villain, and bouncy music. The couple ordered Irish coffees. They suggested that I order an Irish coffee. I tasted the drink, and it made my chest and head expand.

*

On the one-month anniversary of my arrival, I wrote my first letter to my parents. I closed the letter by saying that it was 1 AM, and that I was going to walk to the fruit stand around the corner and buy a plum. I did that often. Walking to the fruit stand around the corner at 1 AM, I was free. I walked with my shoulders back. I was a perfected version of lonely.

*

The man with the handlebar mustache hired me to work at his furniture refinishing shop in the West Village, which was called The Village Stripper. An extremely muscular young man taught me how to strip off old stain and put on new stain and polyurethane coating. His name was Manny, although he let it be known that he did not tell people his last name and that he would turn his back if anyone tried to take his photograph. He seemed to have a cigarette hanging out the right corner of his mouth and a brush—containing either stripper, stain, or polyurethane—in his right hand at all times. He made it clear to me that I was not picking up the techniques of stripping or refinishing very quickly. However, he seemed willing to spend as much time as necessary teaching me.

The man with the handlebar mustache breezed in and out of the shop, telling each of us which project to work on and when it needed to be finished, and giving me extra instruction. By two or three in the afternoon, he would leave for the day. Manny told me that he was at the bar down the street. One day, just at five, he returned to the shop. Manny and I had washed up and were in the front room. He weaved past us and went into the workshop. We followed. The boss grabbed a drawer that Manny had stained; it was drying on the workbench. "What the hell is this?" he said, and dropped the drawer on a table, grabbed a brush, started rummaging through cans of stain, and then threw the brush on the table, hitting the drawer. He swung around and looked at a large, ornate, decorative piece that I was working on.

The piece was meant to serve as a partition in a new restaurant. It was the biggest piece he had ever let me do. I knew it looked ragged at best. There were many gaps in the wood that needed to be concealed with wood filler, but the filler didn't take stain. He let his eyes sweep across the piece. "Jesus fucking Christ." He grabbed the brush again and poked it at several spots on the piece. As if overwhelmed by the scale of its awfulness, he snorted, threw the brush down, and went into the front room, where he fell into the chair behind his desk. At exactly the pace he fell into the chair, a wave of numbness swept my body.

Manny said, "Fucking guy," not loud, but not whispering. He repeated it: "Fucking guy." He had already put on his bright, blue-striped street shirt, and now he put on his jacket. Then he walked out the front door.

I stood in the back room, considering Manny's reaction. It was something I had never considered. Manny was angry. He was angry at the man with the handlebar mustache. There was purity in his anger. Also disgust. When Manny said, "Fucking guy," the man with the handlebar mustache, as I saw him, seemed to wither, became silly, became a child having a tantrum. Manny dismissed him.

In Manny's eyes, there was fault. It was the boss's. And fuck him.

*

On the subway, I stood, leaning with my back against the door. Opposite me, another young man was leaning with his back against a door. He glared at me. Three stops later, I straightened as the door behind me opened. The young man across from me walked toward the opening door, turned his head, spat in my face, and exited the train.

*

The actress who played the hotel landlady in the musical was a friend of the couple who had brought me there. She was at least ten years older than I was. She had dark hair, circles under her eyes concealed with makeup, and a penchant for calling people by their full first names even when they went by nicknames. I understood this habit was an affectation, but it still felt warm and intimate when she called me Robert. One night, after her boyfriend had left her a note saying he was moving to California, she invited me to take a walk. She was sad and that night did not call people by their full names. I felt honored that she wanted to walk with me. I wanted her to feel better. We stopped for hot dogs. I had never liked hot dogs in the past, but these were delicious.

Winter was coming, and as we walked I studied her black wool coat, and her longing and loneliness felt like they were mine.

*

Nighttime. I was walking on the Bowery, a few blocks from my apartment. I liked to walk up and down the Bowery. Everyone I saw seemed lost, maybe near death, yet full of purpose.

I heard a shout from a nearby parking lot: "Get that boy!"

I waited as they ran toward me. My arms and legs were numb, but also, I felt a fitness of things. I liked the heart-thumping of fear. Now something bad was happening. The thumping was harder and so it felt more pleasurable. The bad thing was actually in motion.

Four or five young men surrounded me. The one facing me wore a white t-shirt. He calmly explained that resisting made no sense because they would without hesitation make me sorry I had been born. I gave them my five dollars. As I walked away, I felt limp but peaceful, as though from a job well done.

*

The musical director of the Western play needed a roommate and moved into my apartment. A few days later, we stood in our kitchen, which contained a bathtub, and was the largest room in the apartment. He produced a brown paper bag from somewhere and pulled from it a round carton with an ornate gold design. He pulled open a squeaky drawer and produced an old bread knife and two spoons. After only a few days, he seemed to have mastered where things were kept, while I did not even know that I owned a bread knife. He set the carton on its side and cut across its width. He handed me half the carton and a spoon. When I started the spoon toward the ice cream, he told me to wait, that it needed at least fifteen minutes to soften. The ice cream tasted like rich, sweet coffee. The flavor was like the first part of a trick, the second part of which would involve my being told that what I was eating did not actually exist. My chest and head expanded in joy.

Later, my roommate moved into an apartment across from three Indian restaurants and next to a church. The apartment doorbells did not work. My former roommate instructed me to climb over the church fence, walk up the stairs and around the side of the church, lean over the areaway, and knock on his tall kitchen window. Once, when I got to his window, I saw him standing in his tiny kitchen, naked, juggling. When he saw me, he shrugged and caught the three balls.

*

I sang along with songs on my record player. My roommate had paid one month's rent with a classical guitar, and I learned to play chords. I put an advertisement in the classified section of *The Village Voice* with the headline "Rock and Roll," looking for musicians to form a band, for which I would sing. Among the people answering the ad, a drummer and I enjoyed talked to each other on the phone. He said he liked the wording in my ad, and we had many musical likes in common. I continued working on my singing. I scheduled a rehearsal space with drums and amps, and the musicians and I chose some songs we all knew. The rehearsal space was near the warehouse where my roommate had gotten me a job.

The musicians and I met there one evening. The drummer came with a beautiful girlfriend who would have been right in place at the clubs I went to. He seemed surprised when he saw me—I assumed because I was so young. Everyone set up and plugged in. My mic was connected to an amp. We began our first song. I began singing but couldn't hear myself. I sang louder but still couldn't hear. We tried another song. After that song, I heard the drummer whisper to his girlfriend, "I can't hear him— is he any good?" She shrugged. We went through the songs we had planned, taking a break in the middle. I had reserved the studio for an hour. With about ten minutes left, the owner came in and, sounding a little annoyed, told us we needed to pack up because someone else was coming at the top of the hour. The drummer packed up quickly and, with his girlfriend, left first, saying only, "Hey." Although I had not heard my voice or seen myself in a mirror, I was certain that I had embarrassed myself and that starting a band was a stupid idea and that I would never be able to walk down this street again because of the pain I would feel in my face and head if I passed this building.

*

Besides my roommate, I had one other friend. He often said that he hated things. He made proclamations. My favorite was, "I hate art." However, he liked some things. I was surprised and honored that he apparently liked me. He also liked coffee and cheesecake. He served them to me at his mother's high-rise apartment in Queens. (She was out of town and had left him some money. He told me that he doubted she intended for him to spend the money on coffee and cheesecake.) He made coffee in an old-fashioned percolator. I had never had coffee that tasted so good, and I had never tasted cheesecake, and they both made me throb happily and my head float. After I took the train home, I bought a percolator from a tiny hardware store and the same kind of coffee he had from a tiny grocery store. (I looked at a cheesecake, but I could not conceive of having something so opulent in my refrigerator.)

The first pot of coffee I made in the percolator tasted wonderful. The next time my friend came to my apartment, I made him a pot of coffee, but when I went to pour it, we discovered a cockroach had crawled in. My friend made the same scowl he made when he said he hated something. But then he said he wouldn't let a cockroach ruin a pot of coffee. Still, I knew he wasn't happy with me.

A few months later, my roommate said that my friend called one night when I was out and seemed to be on drugs and said sexual things about me in an aggressive manner. I asked my friend whether he had called me the night before, and he said no. I decided not to think about it. But I felt it, like a layer of blacktop, present.

*

Frequently, when I walked down my street at night, when it was nearly deserted, I would see approaching me in the distance a single figure. I would have to decide whether to continue walking and risk being mugged or to cross the street and walk on the other side. I mentioned this to my friend who hated everything, and he said, "It's cooler to be mugged."

His highest standard and highest praise was "cool."

I yearned for him to respond to my comments with "cool," and I worked very hard formulating each remark to try to achieve that goal, with only rare success. When something wasn't cool—was silly or unsophisticated or insufficiently insightful or vulnerable or childish—he would respond with a sharp glare.

He and I would go out every weekend to see rock groups at CBGB or Max's Kansas City. He would drive his dead father's car to pick me up or meet me outside the club. There, if we encountered a long line, he would say, "That line doesn't apply to us," and walk to the front.

Evenings at the club were long. We would arrive early, at 9 PM or so, to get a seat up front. And we frequently didn't leave until 2 AM. After we had secured our seats, I would follow him back out to his car, where he would produce joints that we would smoke. We repeated the process during breaks between bands and between sets. I loved the music, the way it swept over me, the way it seemed completely new. No one danced. Everyone just sat or stood and watched or tried to talk, the music sweeping over all of us. I longed to listen without the foggy head—worse as the night went on—that my friend's joints created, but I could not refuse his offers.

I never called him to arrange our outings. He always called me. I barely could conceive that of all the people who might be cool in New York, he chose me to go with him. However, it was hard to spend so many hours trying to think of things to say that would earn the response "cool" or at least would avoid the glare. It was easier to be alone and to imagine that each of my observations was worthy. I would rather have gone to see the bands by myself, yet when he called, the honor of being asked, the hope that this time I would hit exactly the right note of cynicism and insight, outweighed my desire to stay home.

Once, on the phone, he said, angrily, "You never call me. I always have to call you."

I did not know what to say, so I said nothing.

*

My mom wrote me a letter. In the letter, she said that when Steve drew pictures of the family, I was no longer included.

I could conjure those pictures in Steve's shaky lines. They were more like his sideview bus drawings, more like a diagram than a picture of a family.

90

But when I envisioned those pictures, they were beautiful because they were drawn by Steve, because they were the anchor of his life, and I was not sure what good I did in the world if I was not his anchor.

*

The old woman was screaming into the telephone. Cursing at someone. She was standing at the phone booth on the corner opposite my apartment building. "Don't think you can treat me that way and get away with it, you fucker," she said.

I was entranced by the raw edge of her screaming. I was glad that she was screaming. I took her side against whomever she was yelling at. I pictured myself screaming.

She slammed the receiver into its cradle. Then she picked it back up and continued screaming. She slammed it down. She picked it up and continued to scream.

I wanted to be on the phone, screaming at no one.

*

Standing on a crowded train platform, trains wailing past, I was anonymous. I could do anything. No repercussions. I could walk quickly back and forth through the crowd, dodging people with deft footwork. I could sing part of a song, even one that my friend who hated things would glare at. I could practice: my polite and friendly look, my overwhelmed-by-life look, my deeply thoughtful look, my tough look. I could practice a posture that was me as tall as my true stature.

*

On a bright Friday summer afternoon, I was walking through Central Park. I had just been paid, in cash, and had been on my way to reward myself by buying five dollars' worth of marijuana, which came in a tiny brown envelope.

In an instant, one person blocked my way, while I felt another pressing against me from behind. The one in front put one of his hands in each of my front pockets, and the other did the same with my back pockets.

I felt a sense that events were transpiring exactly as they should and each of us was playing his role correctly.

*

Walking, I was pushing forward as though through knee-deep water. Or perhaps more to the point, when I walked between tall buildings, they impeded my progress by their very presence, creating a denseness of air I had to constantly expend noticeable effort to traverse. I attributed this in part to the denseness of detail in the city that drew attention intently and constantly. However, it was also a physical sensation. Walking through knee-deep water. The beautiful impediments of a big city.

*

I walked the three blocks from my apartment to CBGB. It was Wednesday, a quiet night. A young woman with huge wavy hair began talking with me. We talked about music, about where she was from, about me. Her face was wide. Her mouth was wide. When I looked at her face and her hair and her long, worn tweed coat, I thought of a comfortable bed.

We left the club and began to walk. Eventually, we arrived in a small park, where we sat. We stopped talking. I assumed that I was supposed to kiss her, and I did. I was not sure how to kiss, but I tried to do it in a way that carried the sense I felt of her, the sense of comfort and softness. She put her arms around me. The feeling was earnest, warm, unknown.

We kissed and hugged for a long time. Sometimes we paused and then began again. We paused and sat in silence and talked a little more and kissed and hugged again. I waited for her to say that she had to go. But she did not say it. As the sky began to show signs of light, I peed against a tree trunk, and we started to walk again. I asked about seeing her again. She said she would be at CBGB in two nights.

Just in case, I went to CBGB the next night. I saw her at the far side of the room, talking with a man with long wavy hair. He looked very confident. They were laughing. She touched the lapels of his jacket. I went home.

I went to CBGB the night we were supposed to meet. I waited there for two hours, but she did not appear.

*

My roommate got me a job with him at a warehouse, and soon I was a hand-truck expert. I was in command of my hand truck. I used my hand truck with authority. I tipped the upper part of the hand truck forward, against a stack of boxes, tipping the stack back just enough to create a tiny space at very bottom. I slid the blade into that space, put my hand on the top of the stack, and rocked the stack back into the hand truck. I continued that motion, pulling back on the hand truck by the handles, and I was ready to wheel the stack of boxes anywhere. The process was easier with a stack of new boxes with rigid sides. The process was harder when the boxes were worn and spongy. Yet I was a master. I could scoop even the spongiest stack of boxes in one smooth motion, accompanied by a satisfyingly crisp scrape of the metal blade on the concrete floor, then scoot the stack into the narrowest opening and remove the hand truck with another authoritative scrape. This is how I imagined dancing felt.

I was also an expert at sliding my way through crowds on the street. People here walked fast, but I walked faster.

*

My boss led me up a dark staircase to the mezzanine of the warehouse. He wore a blindingly white shirt of thick, starched cotton with monogrammed cuffs and large black-and-silver cuff links. A fragrance came off him that made me wonder if I had eaten too much of a rich meal.

94

On the mezzanine, I saw a small printing press with a hand crank. Sheet music was strewn on various surfaces, and more sheet music was stacked on wooden shelves that, even at a distance, seemed ready to give me a splinter.

My boss gestured toward the sheet music; his gesture said at once "this is nothing special" and "this is my life's work."

His accent sounded to me like Dracula in a cartoon. He said, "I write marches for every president since Roosevelt. I write marches for Eisenhower, for Nixon."

On the table by the printer, I saw the title "The First Lady Waltz" for Pat Nixon.

He said, "They give a concert of my work in Central Park. They say the bullshit, that I am the next Sousa." I saw a record album with the title *The Common Ground* in large letters and a photograph of Eisenhower and Khrushchev shaking hands.

I wondered who bought all this sheet music, or whether perhaps he just sent it to people unsolicited. And why sheet music? Why not recordings? His white shirt, his cufflinks, his cologne seemed to signal a will, a forcefulness—something that I, too, might have.

He leaned toward me, looking conspiratorial. He growled, "I will not write a march for President Carter, even if they ask me."

*

Oh, how I loved picking up *The Village Voice* at the newsstand by the train station every Wednesday after work. Oh, how I loved spreading it open—even while shouldering my way through the people on the stairs and on the platform—to the nightclub section and all those box ads seeming to blink at me: Television (before and after Richard Hell left), Tuff Darts, Mumps (with Lance Loud and Kristian Hoffman of An American Family— nobody sweated on stage like Lance), Marbles, The Miamis (oh, to be half as clever and happy as the Wynbrandt brothers), The Dolls (formerly The New York Dolls, now performing without Johnny and Arthur and Jerry, but with Chris Robison (soon replaced by Bobby Blain) and Tony Machine and Peter Jordan, (whom I chatted with where he worked at Bleeker Bob's record store), the Ramones (my favorite moment was when they started playing a song and a minute later the guitarist and bass player realized they were playing two different songs and started shouting at each other), Talking Heads (I sometimes sat near David Byrne at CBGB), Blondie, Richard Hell and the Voidoids, Stumblebunny, Harry Toledo, Wayne County and the Backstreet Boys, The Heartbreakers, The Criminals, The Dictators, The Fast.

No one had a better life than I did.

*

My roommate and I were in the living room. I was reading. He was eating from a plate on his lap. I put down the book. My roommate said, "What's wrong?"

I said, "What?"

He said, "What's wrong?"

I said, "Nothing."

I did not know what was wrong, but I trusted my roommate's

observational abilities. So something must have been wrong. And if something were wrong at this ordinary moment, that meant something must have been wrong all the time.

*

One winter day, I was walking down Avenue A. I was wearing a tweed coat, bought from a rag vendor who pushed a wagon in the West Village, over an old leather jacket. I was about three blocks from my apartment and eager to get out of the cold when I heard yells, and with blurry speed I was surrounded.

When I was able to focus on the people surrounding me, I saw that they were shorter than I was. Nobody was shorter than I was. They were bouncing and yelling. They were kids. Probably only two or three years younger than I was, but still—kids.

The one blocking my path said, "Gimme your money or I'll cut you." He waved something near my face that looked like a small knife. I felt good that the stakes of my muggings had risen to the level of a knife but disappointed that the knife-wielder was so young.

I had only three dollars. I didn't want to get stabbed. But they were kids. I was only two blocks from my apartment. This was my neighborhood. And I wanted to see what would happen.

I said, "No."

"Gimme your money." The others continued to yelp and jump around. We were standing in the middle of the sidewalk. People looked, but no one stopped.

With a tone of scorn that surprised me, I said, "I'm not giving my money to you." I put some emphasis on the word "you."

One of the kids kicked me on the chin. I wondered how he was able to get his leg that high. The first kid waved the knife. "Gimme. Your. Money."

"I'll tell you what," I said. I reached under my coat and pulled the three dollars out of my pocket. "I'll give you one dollar." I separated it from the other two and handed it to him.

He snatched it out of my hand and jabbed the knife into my arm around the bicep. I didn't notice any signal, but the gang ran off, bouncing and whooping.

I looked at my arm, but couldn't tell how far the knife had penetrated through the coat and jacket. My chin felt sore.

I watched them recede, then resumed my walk. I had found something—the point where logic turned off, where powerlessness turned off. As I walked the last blocks home, it seemed to me my instincts were strong and pure.

When I entered my apartment, I saw that the window off the fire escape was open and my stereo was gone.

*

On the warehouse floor, a young man approached me. He was tall, muscular, wearing a tight t-shirt with a team logo that I did not recognize, and tight jeans. His face was dominated by a sharp jaw and sharp cheekbones. I suspected that he was going to identify something I was doing wrong. He leaned down so his eyes were in line with mine and asked, his voice surprisingly gentle, "Where are you from?"

It occurred to me that the question was understandable. I didn't look like anyone else here—I was shorter than anyone else, younger than anyone else; I was the only person with blond hair and glasses with silly black frames. Try as I did to have the New York growl and accent of my friend who hated everything, I knew that I sounded different from anyone else. My jeans came from a rag vendor, and I wore the same pair every day. I wore the same dirty-white tennis shoes every day, and I was pretty sure they smelled bad.

Yet answering this question was complicated. Peoria. The name sounded like a whine. The city had long been the butt of jokes, or at best, a symbol of all that is unremarkable. It was true: Everything in Peoria was flat, everything was gray, everything was medium-sized, everything was sad. I felt so sorry for my father, although he seemed to have adjusted—sorry that he had grown up in storybook Brooklyn and ended up in Peoria. I imagined him meeting fellow artists on visits to New York and having to answer the question, "Where do you live?" and facing up bravely to having to answer, "Peoria." I knew that, to my mother, Peoria was a daily horror of classlessness and mediocrity, an indictment of all her values of aesthetics and behavior. Peoria was the city that gave her Steve—and Steve's dead brother.

I believed that it was not possible for anyone—no matter how talented, how confident, how worldly, how famous—to lose the stain of Peoria. Peoria would always be there, needing attention every day in order to be tamped down and hidden, eating away at whatever confidence anyone would be able to present to the world. That twitch of doubt in a charismatic person's smile: That would be Peoria.

I did not have a ready answer to the young man's question. I did not want to lie; that would have doubled my embarrassment.

Looking at him, thinking about his gentle voice, seeing that he had even leaned over to be at my level, I thought that perhaps telling him the truth would result in little damage.

I said, "Peoria, Illinois."

"Peoria." He straightened up. A huge, delighted smile opened. "Peoria?" His voice was louder. He turned toward the rest of the warehouse floor. "Hey, he's from Peoria!" He began to laugh, and the group next to us began to laugh, and the laughter spread, and soon everyone on the warehouse floor was laughing.

I felt blank. As the laughter began to diminish, the young man turned to me, slapped me on the shoulder, and said, "You're OK."

The next day he offered to share some of his angel dust with me after work.

*

I stood at a long counter. Rows of record albums, mouths up, spines down, rested in front of me. I could only see the cover of the album at the front of each row. Otherwise, all I could see were the small gaps of the mouths, held together with barely visible shrink wrap. I held a mat knife, blade protruding. I went down the rows, from closest to farthest, rapidly cutting a tiny slice in the shrink wrap along the slit of each album's mouth. When all the cuts were made, I set down the knife. I grasped each mouth at the slit, right thumb at the upper lip and left index finger at the lower lip, and I pulled the mouth apart, ripping apart the plastic wrap. I went quickly—this was assembly-line-type work, and speed was valued—but I enjoyed the faint sound, like a wave coming ashore in a fast-motion film. Once all the mouths were freed, I grasped each album at the sides and slid the plastic wrap off. For some albums, the plastic would come off in one or two strokes. For others, when the plastic was especially thick, or especially thin, or when it stuck to the album jacket, it was hard to slide off. A few weeks before, I had written an article for a tiny music magazine about the different quality of plastic of different albums, naming the albums. Someone responded that it was clever of me to use the plastic to describe the music, but that was not my intent at all. I had never heard the music. I just wanted to describe the plastic. This was my favorite task, and I would do it all day, every day, if I were allowed.

*

The letter from my dad said, "Your mother spent a few days in the hospital, and now she no longer takes sleeping pills."

I rarely saw Dad and Mom speak to one another. Not, I thought, because of any animosity between them; they were both busy with their own projects, or they were silently focused on Steve. However, I always assumed that Dad and Mom spoke when they were together, in the evening, when Dad came up from his work in the basement and when Mom emerged from her studio or office. I imagined that they talked about art. I imagined that they talked about Steve's schooling. I imagined they complained about how difficult I was.

Reading this bare line of Dad's letter, the only line that referred to Mom's condition, I thought again about the two of them together, alone. Dad usually worked late in the basement. Probably on most nights when he came upstairs, Mom was asleep—or, more precisely, passed out from sleeping pills and beer.

Perhaps Dad had decided to come upstairs early one night to speak with her. Perhaps, when he entered the bedroom, Mom was drunk and about to take a sleeping pill. Perhaps Dad said, "LaVerne, we need to talk about your sleeping pills. I'm worried about you." And perhaps he slowly persuaded her that she needed help, and she eventually acquiesced.

As soon as this scene ran through my mind, another more likely one took its place. Dad, in the basement, heard several thumps from above. He waited, then heard a sound like a table or a lamp—or both—hitting the floor. He trotted upstairs. He looked in Steve's room. He was in bed. He trotted down the hall. In their bedroom, Mom was lying across the bed. She was clothed. She was muttering. Dad said, "LaVerne!" There were no pet names in our house. He grabbed her shoulders and said, louder, putting his face in front of Mom's, whose head had lolled to one side, "LaVerne!" He wanted to slap her into consciousness but couldn't bring himself to. He wanted to slap her because he was angry. He grasped her shoulders and shook her, as he had that evening when I had summoned him to help Mom as she wobbled up the stairs. She didn't respond. He called an ambulance. In the hospital, the next morning, with Dad standing to one side, a doctor told Mom—told, didn't ask—that she would be staying in the hospital for several days, and that they would make her as comfortable as possible while she got used to life without sleeping pills.

Or maybe none of this happened.

I wondered where Steve was when Mom and Dad were at the hospital. Probably in the room, trying to get away from Dad's grip, so he could run up and down the gleaming white halls.

*

I closed my apartment and started toward the staircase. Before I reached it, the woman across the hall opened her door.

It was the middle of the day. She was wearing a nightgown and holding a garbage bag. The hall, always dark, felt darker than usual. I pictured the lady inside all day.

Meeting my eyes, she smiled broadly. "There he is! My singing cowboy!" I waved from my waist and continued down the stairs.

I did not realize that people could hear me attempting to learn how to strum songs. I would play and sing more quietly.

*

My parents visited with Steve. They invited me to see the Twyla Tharp Dance Company. I was sitting next to my mom. Steve escaped and started to run down the aisle toward the stage. I captured him and eased him back.

A couple walking up the aisle stopped, and the man addressed my dad. It seemed he was a painter my dad had hosted once at our university. My dad introduced me. The man said to me, "Do you like ballet?"

Before I could answer, my mom said, "All he cares about is

rock music at those downtown nightclubs."

The lights went down. During the performance, I felt my face getting hot. I was vibrating. I began rehearsing. When the first portion of the performance ended and the lights came up, I turned to my mom, my words ready. She looked at me as though she knew what was coming.

"Why would you say that about me?" My voice was trembling. "Why would you criticize me like that in public? I'm a straight-A student. I read literature. I play piano. But I have never, not once, heard you say anything nice about me."

She said, "I didn't want you to get a swelled head."

*

After working and then going to CBGB three nights in a row, I fainted—it felt more like falling asleep while moving—as I brought food from a local deli into CBGB for my friend who hated everything. When I opened my eyes, looking down at me was one of my musical heroes, Syl Sylvain of The New York Dolls, who had recently broken his leg in a car accident. "Hey man," he said, "do you want my crutches?" He was smiling, and I thought he would be a good father.

I also thought this would be a good story to tell my friend who hated everything, who was waiting for me at a table. Surely this story would warrant a "cool." He smiled at the story but didn't like the food that I brought for us to eat.

*

On subway rides, I looked at reflections of beautiful girls. Sometimes I thought they were looking back at me, but it was hard to tell because of the angles of the reflections. But I hoped that they did look back at me sometimes.

*

My friend who hated everything never clapped at music shows and I didn't either because I wanted to be like him and to have his respect. But I felt bad because I wanted all those musicians trying so hard to know how much I appreciated their efforts, knowing that for most of them their time in front of a crowd was fleeting and they should get all the applause they could.

*

A new guy at work invited me to hang out with him one Saturday in Queens. I went to his apartment, met his wife, and then he and I walked. It was sunny. Unlike in Manhattan, here I could see sky. We sat on a park bench. We got some lunch. We walked more and chatted. The blankness of the sun, the blankness of the landscape, seemed to erase the day, to erase sensations. I didn't know what to talk about. I was panicked that the day would not end.

*

At work, everyone called me Bobby. This was not even close to the name that I preferred, but no one here showed any interest in what I liked to be called. Also, I accepted the name because I knew it reflected how young and small I was.

My friend who hates things called me Rock, which I took to be a reference to our shared musical interest and also an ironic comment about how young and small I was.

*

Laryssa was the new junior accountant. Although I was a warehouse worker, I had a desk in the administrative area, and I went in and out with bills of lading from shipments.

Laryssa was five or ten years older than I was. She was very thin. After a few exchanges, I realized that I had seen a picture of her before. She used to be a background singer for an underground New York rock band I had read about, and I had stared and stared at the picture of the band, particularly the background singers, who looked ordinary, except that they wore skimpy and sparkly costumes, feather boas, and elbow-length gloves.

Without the costume, at work, she was calm and serious. We would chat about things—books, music—and even laugh. It was a relief to talk with someone besides my friend who hated everything, to be able to express a thought or opinion without flinching against the inevitable response. Yet whenever we talked, I always knew one thing: that she was wiser than I was.

A salesman gave her two tickets to a movie premier, and she asked if I wanted to go. I had not heard of the film, but when we arrived by cab—a rare luxury—I saw that the showing was at a glitzy mid-town theater. Inside, every seat appeared to be full.

The film began. It was a space adventure. A great big live-action boy's adventure. The Power Boys in space. The screen was huge, and the images enveloped me. The hero was a slim, blond boy. He was also a gifted pilot. He left home to fight with the rebel warriors. He was good. They were bad. There were clever robots, a world-weary but courageous pilot, and a princess.

Laryssa and I giggled and poked each other at the corniness of the film. Yet I also loved it. I didn't so much watch it as live within it. In the culminating battle scene, the hero navigated through cream-colored troughs, narrow and angular, barely avoiding disaster at each turn.

I slumped in my seat and leaned into Laryssa. "This is the best movie I have ever seen," I said. The comment was meant to be ironic, but also it was true.

When the heroes returned to their planet after defeating the evil forces, the movie lingered as they were unreservedly celebrated, praised, cheered. I hid that I was crying. When the movie was over, Laryssa squeezed my shoulder, and I felt enormously privileged that she, this wise person I could say things to, would squeeze my arm, even if it was just a signal to stand up.

In the cab, I leaned back and felt a sensation that I had once heard described as the cool of the evening.

*

I was sitting in my apartment, watching a cop show on my small television. The TV went off. The lights went off. I looked out the window. No lights in the buildings nearby or outside. I used the gas burners for light but soon turned them off and went to bed.

In the morning, the power was still out. I took the bus to work. There, I was told that the power was out all over the city. I worked for a couple of hours and then left. Everywhere, people were sitting on stoops, walking. It was a bright summer day. Restaurants had their doors open, and people seemed to be moving in and out of them as they would a train station. I went inside one coffee shop. I saw piles of egg boxes and rows of frying eggs on the griddle. The restaurants seemed to be giving away food.

At home that evening, families had set up chairs on the sidewalks. Kids were everywhere. The grown-ups were chatting. Strangers talked to strangers. The kids shouted and spun. I didn't care if the power ever came on.

*

When Laryssa was not at work two days in a row, I asked the elderly office manager where Laryssa was. The office manager stubbed out a cigarette and told me that Laryssa was very sick, that she was in the hospital, that she probably wouldn't be back. I asked which hospital, and the office manager, seeming annoyed, said she didn't know.

At home after work, I took out the business telephone book. I sat on the padded seat next to the telephone and opened the phone book to the listing of hospitals. The newsprint pages felt tacky to my fingertips; the type looked messy and grim. I called the first hospital and asked if it had anyone named Laryssa Wachuta registered. No. I tried the next hospital. No. I got a pencil so I could mark off the hospitals as I called them. I continued. No. No. No. The room was getting darker, and I turned on a table lamp. The light made the list of hospitals look even more inky and tired. I called every hospital in New York. She was registered at none of them.

*

On my eighteenth birthday, I went to a liquor store and bought a small bottle of rye whiskey. I didn't really want it, but I wanted to be asked for my identification and to be of age. The clerk didn't ask for my identification. I went to a movie.

*

The phone rang in my grandparents' apartment.

I was visiting, as I did every other Sunday. I sat at the kitchen table and talked for hours with my grandmother. My grandfather didn't say much. He mostly sat in his easy chair in the living room and watched ballgames or read paperback books that he kept in plastic covers and in which he marked his place with rubber bands.

I didn't recall ever hearing the phone ring here before. The sound was sharp and seemed to come from an older time, as if it were being transported from a black-and-white movie.

My grandfather's chair was close to the phone, and I heard him say "hello" in his high, scratchy, confused-sounding voice.

After a few seconds, he called, "Anna." His voice seemed to rise while he was saying the name. My grandma and I walked into the living room.

"It's LaVerne," he said, pronouncing my mom's name the way he always did, "LaVoyne." His face looked foggy. He was holding the receiver toward my grandmother. His hand trembled.

She looked at my grandfather with some annoyance, took the receiver, pulled it toward her against the counterforce of the coiled cord, and held it to her ear as if the act were unfamiliar. "Hello? LaVerne?"

She listened for a few seconds. She said, as though translating words from another language, "Gerald is dead?" She screamed and threw the receiver, the recoiling cord making the receiver travel as though under its own power.

1977-1980

Mom, Paul, and Steve were in our car, pulled up to the curb. My mother was in the driver's seat. Paul was next to her. Steve and I were in the back seat.

Mom asked, "Do you want to go in?" directing the question to Paul and me.

Paul immediately said yes. I was surprised. Paul was rather quiet, rather passive. This seemed to take courage. I was proud of him.

The world was still. There seemed to be no people, no other cars, no other activity. It wasn't so much an absence of activity as a suspension of it, as though the world had inhaled and was not yet ready to breathe out.

I thought about what my dad would look like, in his coffin, in some room in the funeral home, waiting to be cremated. I imagined his face as the last black-and-white photo I had seen of him, wearing his favorite jacket, his hair full, his sideburns turning gray. Mom had already told me that he would be cremated wearing that same jacket. I imagined that I would first see him from the side, just his nose and perhaps a bit of his forehead or cheek or chin. As I got closer, I would see more of his profile, but never his full face, because I would not be able to go that close, to look down at him. He would look like that photo, with makeup applied to transform him from black-

and-white to an artificial-looking color. Except he would not be smiling. And his eyes would be closed. And he would be lying on his back. And he would be in a box. And he would never move.

I pictured the people every day who lined up to look down at bodies in coffins. It seemed to me that everyone in the world did this, particularly when the dead body is a loved one's. It is the chance to say goodbye. A normal person, a courageous person, any person would want to look at that parent or spouse or child one last time and say goodbye.

I said, "No."

They got out of the car. I sat there alone. They came back in about ten minutes. I studied their faces. Mom was crying. Steve was wiggling to get away from mom's hand holding his arm. Paul's face was more deeply blank than any face I had ever seen.

Mom drove away, but somehow I felt like I was driving the car.

*

Paul wrote something fairly long for Dad's posthumous art catalogue. I declined. Paul made thoughtful remarks at Dad's memorial service. I read a short passage from a book but added no words of my own. I was conscious that I enjoyed being in front of an audience, which I accepted as a damning indictment.

After the memorial service, a woman told me that the friends of my family were really my father's friends and not my mother's friends.

Mom's father and his wife visited, separately. They left, and we were alone.

*

Paul reclined on the living room sectional and read the paper.

I watched TV with Steve. We watched his favorite shows: *Mister Rodger's Neighborhood*, *Sesame Street*, *The Electric Company*, and *Zoom*. We watched these shows every day. The repetition, the modest variations within familiar structures, was comforting.

*

Mom took me into her bedroom and opened my dad's bottom dresser drawer. From under a pile of folded sweaters, she withdrew a book with a black cover and handed it to me. It was a book about how to be a better lover. I loved my dad very much at that moment.

Mom asked for my help to write a check. She said she did not know how to fill out a check. This was flat-out untrue. I had seen Mom make out dozens of checks. I helped her, but impatiently.

Mom smelled bad.

Before, when Mom sat on the couch, she seemed to pose, to depict relaxation. Now she seemed to be falling through the cushion.

Sometimes Mom would sit on the living room floor, leaning

against the couch. She would look up at Paul, reading the paper, and say, "You have such a good heart." She would turn to me but not say anything.

*

I called the teacher who wore the paperclip on his collar, and we met in his office. I talked quite a bit about books and about my time in New York. Toward the end, he said, laughing, "Well, one thing you got from New York was a New York accent." Embarrassment throbbed in my arms and my chest. I was using the voice of my New York friend who hated everything, thinking I could do that here, in Peoria, with impunity.

*

On Christmas morning, we gathered in the living room. Mom sat, sunk into the couch, a glass of orange juice in her hand. Paul reclined on the couch with the morning newspaper. Steve looked at a city map and occasionally ran up the stairs and down. I crouched on the floor, ready to hand out presents from under the tree.

On all sides of us were walls on which hung paintings by Mom, featuring people in silhouette and shadow, and by Dad, featuring brushstrokes that could have been fields on fire with gentle, inviting flames.

When everything under the tree had been distributed, unwrapped, and commented on, Paul left the room to get, he said, his present for Mom.

He returned, arms full of and body covered by the latest product of a painting class he was taking: a large canvas featuring simple, boldly colored geometric figures and, just to the right and below center, one large drip.

He stood in front of the tree and displayed the painting. Mom said thank you. Paul rested the painting against a wall, behind some other presents.

The festivities over, Paul went into the kitchen. Steve looked at a new map. Mom remained on the couch. I stood, unsure of my role now.

Mom looked up at me. "What does he mean, giving me that?"

I was torn between cherishing Mom's confidence and not wanting to hear what came next.

She said, "Every painting he shows me is a different style. What is that thing? Geometric abstraction and one abstract expressionist drip?"

She waved the hand holding the orange juice, dismissing the painting.

Paul returned, resumed his seat on the opposite sofa, and picked up the paper.

Several minutes later, Mom said, "Did I get any presents?" She looked at me. "What did you get me?"

I told her.

"Oh, yes," she said.

Next I named the present that Steve and I had bought for her.

"Oh, yes," she said.

She looked at Paul. "What did you get me?"

He said, "You don't remember?"

Mom let her gaze wander across the presents on the floor and then around the room. "What?"

Paul repeated, "You don't remember?"

Mom said, "You didn't get me anything."

Paul, having committed the crime of not yet finding his style as an artist, left the room, his footsteps heavy on the hardwood floor.

*

When Dad's mother died, we returned to Brooklyn. At the synagogue, I hung back with Steve. I did not want to see my grandmother in her coffin. Even from the back of the room, however, I could see her prominent nose sticking up over the casket. I began trying to craft this image into an anecdote that would be both sad and funny.

My grandfather was sitting Shiva next to an old man I did not know. The man patted my grandfather's thigh. I had never seen anyone touch my grandfather, nor had I seen my grandfather touch anyone else. The idea of someone touching his thigh bordered on just plain wrong, like turning on the cold water tap and having hot water come out.

I had rarely heard my grandfather talk, except to ask, "How long was the drive, Gerald?" when we would arrive for a visit and, after my dad replied, to say, "You made good time, Gerald."

Now Grandpa turned to the man next to him and said, "I feel so bad."

Grandpa wanted to sit Shiva longer, but my mom and others

encouraged him to come home with us. This seemed to me an indignity, that he was not allowed to mourn the way he chose. Would could happen? Could he feel tired? Could he feel stiff and sore? Could he fall off his seat? Could he die? In what way were any of those things something that needed to be avoided at this moment?

At Grandma and Grandpa's apartment, I got on the phone. I talked with the agent of a New York musician I wanted to interview for a book I planned to write. I thought that maybe he and I could meet while I was here. I had already written the first chapter. The agent said she would have the musician call me back, but I could tell by her voice that she wouldn't and he wouldn't.

I always had a project going. Projects were exciting. Projects were shiny objects I reached toward and knew I would grasp. I felt shabby for thinking about my project, for not living within the sadness of the death of someone I loved.

That evening, I heard my mother saying in a loud voice, "Charley! Charley!"

Charley was my grandpa's name. Mom always called Dad's parents by their first names: Anna and Charley. I always found that odd, somehow condescending, as though my mom were a society woman, holding a cigarette in a cigarette holder and talking to some guests she had to treat politely but who made her feel slightly uncomfortable. However, Mom painted large, sad paintings that featured shadowy versions of my dad's parents, which seemed incongruous with her calling them by their first names.

I stepped out of the back bedroom. The voice continued,

coming from the bathroom. I heard sounds of water sloshing. I cracked open the bathroom door. Grandpa was sitting in the bathtub. Mom was leaning over, her hands grasping him from behind, under his armpits. His chest was skeletal. His skin was wrinkled, but beautiful and strong, despite—or perhaps because of—his helplessness.

Mom glanced toward me. "I'm OK. Charley's just having trouble getting out of the tub."

My mother, too, looked beautiful and strong.

*

In the Peoria record store, behind the long counter, a girl was in motion. She was walking away from me. She paused, stretched hard to put something on a high shelf, turned, and headed back toward the front of the store.

Since I had last been here, racks and displays had been slightly rearranged. Different posters were on the wall. I felt that I was wrong, or the place was wrong, or that I just didn't belong there. The girl, too, seemed wrong—too young, too bouncy, for a place that used to employ people who never smiled.

The girl wore a loose-fitting white oxford shirt, a beige vest, a man's tie, and a black bowler hat. Reddish brown hair fell out from under the hat. She was tiny, thin, overwhelmed by the clothing. She walked as though her shoes were made of rubber balls. Her cheeks were round. Her chin was round and dimpled. Beneath the floppy shirt, her shoulders looked round.

Her outfit was a direct match for the main character in a popular movie by a respected director. It was a character I found so irritating—flighty, ungrounded, chirpy, self-centered—that I could barely finish watching the movie.

I waited by the cash register, and the girl met me there. I asked about ordering a record by a fairly obscure musician I used to see in New York.

She said she knew who I was. She said my name. She said that she'd read my articles. We chatted for a moment. She felt light and friendly. In her outfit, she looked like a clown on her day off. She reminded me of the woman in the bar car on the train, the off-duty clown, blowing up balloons, flirting with all the men.

That the girl knew my name made me feel urbane. Like I could occupy a position of some stature here in Peoria.

We talked until I felt as though I had drunk more water than I was used to drinking.

The girl's name was Becky Best. The alliteration made me uncomfortable. She said she painted and when she signed her paintings, she inserted her middle initial so her name sounded more serious.

*

My mom entered my room holding something shiny and gold. I was lying on my back in bed, reading. Mom sat on the side of the bed. She held out the gold object. She told me that it was her Phi Beta Kappa pin, that it was one of the most valuable things she owned, that she wanted me to have it.

I held it gingerly. I felt its value, its importance. I felt the weight of the effort my mom had expended to get it, the confirmation of her intellect, her specialness.

I thanked her and set it on my nightstand.

Two days later, Mom asked to see the pin. I went into my room, approached my nightstand. I felt through the tumble of stuff. I didn't see it. I looked on the floor. I looked on my dresser. I looked on every flat surface. I didn't see it. My mom stood in my doorway.

"I give you something so important to me, and you lose it. That tells me what you think of me."

I did not understand where it had gone. I wondered if Mom was right. I knew I would look for the pin forever and that I would not find it and that the pin would join the collection of things that, whenever I thought of them, would make me feel as though I were falling.

*

I went back to the record store, but Becky wasn't there. I went back again, and she was—looking as though she were perfectly happy without me.

I waited at the counter, and she came over. I knew one of her high school friends—a friend of a friend—and we talked about him, and she mentioned her high school friends and her college plans.

She went to wait on a customer, and I was faintly jealous. She came back, and I felt rewarded.

I mentioned that a singer I liked was playing at a town an hour and a half away—the town where she would be going to college. I said my older brother and I were going. She said she'd love to see the show. I offered to give her a ride, and she immediately said yes.

I cleaned out my car. On the way down, she sat next to me on the bench seat, and Paul sat next to her. She wore a checked short-sleeved shirt with the sleeves rolled up once. I was conscious of her arms, so foreign, so near me.

After the show, I got in the driver's seat, and Paul slid across the passenger side to sit next to me.

Becky said, "Hey, I want to sit next to him." She wanted to sit next to me. She wanted to sit next to me. When we pulled into the highway, she said she was tired and lay her head on my shoulder. She chose me to lean on when she was tired. She wanted to touch me. I wondered how I should behave if I were in love.

*

Mom came home regularly with a paper bag with a gallon-sized bottle in it. She had no other bags, so she'd been to the liquor store, not the grocery store.

Mom told me that my dad was glad when I moved out, that there was less turmoil in the house.

Mom told me that my dad told her that he wanted to have sex with her more often, that he had started masturbating.

Mom told me that she heard me saying over and over "I don't care." I wanted to tell her I was singing a song by that name from the new album by The Ramones, but I thought, well, yes, I had chosen that song to sing.

I wanted Mom to stop telling me things.

I moved into the basement. I kept the desk where Dad used to pay bills, grade assignments, and do taxes. I moved his film editing equipment to a back part of the basement. In its place, I put a bed. I put my stereo next to the bed. The house had a side entrance, from the driveway, that could be used to go a few steps up to the kitchen or directly down to the basement.

*

Becky showed me a picture of one of her high school friends. His name was Rick, she said. In the picture, he was sitting on a bed. The picture was taken from behind. His head was turned slightly to the left, so he was caught in one-quarter profile. She said she liked that picture because it showed his true nature, that he was always on his way somewhere.

*

My friend Dena and I were driving. We had been watching her brother's band practicing in a garage. I tapped my hand on the dashboard as I drove. At the corner, I stopped, looked both ways, and started to make a right turn. My body ricocheted left and then flew to the right. I asked Dena if she was OK. I got out of the car. The driver of the car I had run into was standing beside her car. She was crying. "It was a brand-new car," she said.

Later, she said the same thing to the police officer. "You can get it fixed," he said.

"They're never the same," she said.

"That's an old wives' tale," he said. "You really can fix things as good as new."

Two days later, while I was asleep in the basement, I heard the doorbell ring. I saw light through the tiny windows at the top of the basement wall. I looked at my clock. It was just after six. I went to the door and opened it. A man on the porch opened the screen door. He was only a few years older than I was. He wore a white shirt and an off-center tie. His hair looked like what I imagined mine looked like, having just gotten out of bed. He asked if I was Robert Fromberg, and I said yes. He handed me a thick envelope and left.

Inside were many papers. The top one said I was being sued for $50,000.

My head and chest and legs throbbed. I also felt exactly right in the world.

*

Becky and I entered the side door of my house and walked down the stairs. I turned on the dim light in the laundry room, which gave us just enough light not to bump into things. We kissed. We removed our clothes. We hugged and caressed each other. As I entered her, I hoped I would not embarrass myself. In a minute or two, I orgasmed. I thought that was probably all right. We held each other, talked in quiet voices. I went to the bathroom to pee. Then she went. She dressed and left.

I put on a shirt and my underpants. I was about to put on my pants when I heard the floor above me creak and the door from the stairs to the kitchen open. I tossed the covers over my bed. I walked up the stairs and met my mom on the landing.

"Are you alone?" she asked.

"Becky was here before. Now I'm getting ready for bed."

She looked me up and down. "You are so handsome," she said.

I didn't reply.

She looked me up and down again. "Your shoulders are so broad. You are so handsome."

I walked back downstairs.

*

Mom started teaching classes at a community arts center. Painting. Two classes per week. But sometimes the phone would ring, and it would be someone from the arts center telling her she had missed one of her classes.

*

In the living room, Mom asked me to find her glasses. I picked them up from the coffee table. Mom turned them over, studying them. She said they weren't her glasses; maybe they were mine. I pointed to my glasses, told her that I was wearing mine. She looked at the pair in her hand again. "Nope," she said, "not mine."

*

I called a family acquaintance, a psychiatrist, and arranged an appointment for Mom. I told her about the appointment. I said I thought it would help her. She and I were sitting at the kitchen table. Her skin seemed to get darker. She looked down at the Formica surface.

I drove her to the small office building and dropped her off. She walked in with her head down. I parked and sat in the waiting room. She came out a half hour later. She walked past me quickly, shaking. The nurse gave me a prescription. Mom did not look at me or talk as we drove. Her silence said to me, "You betrayed me." At home, she went upstairs and shut the door of her bedroom.

I was terrified. I went to the drug store to fill the prescription. I hurried. The medicine would help.

I gave Mom the bottle of pills. The next day she was shaking. Shaking hard. "It's the pills," she said. I took her to the emergency room. She came out of the examination room shaking less. She didn't take the pills anymore, and she didn't go back to the psychiatrist.

*

Becky's mother was a nurse. She had a high voice. Her mouth trembled slightly when she drew on a cigarette. Her husband worked at the Pabst Blue Ribbon canning plant. He had a lovely, closed-lips smile. When he chuckled, as he did often, the chuckle quavered slightly. They met in Peoria's mental hospital, after both having nervous breakdowns. I thought they were the loveliest people I had ever met. I felt that I could sit with them at their kitchen table, chatting, forever.

*

Becky told me that Rick was a brilliant person but that he couldn't be pinned down. She said she and Rick had had sex twice. She said he was the only boy she had had sex with before me. She said she liked me better because I was steadier. Or maybe she said dependable. In other words, I was the slightly more boring but less difficult alternative to the brilliant boy she really wanted.

*

A teacher in a literature class asked us how we would describe someone we loved. One student said, "Someone you want to live with, to marry." The teacher said, "Oh, no. You may love someone and not be able to live with him." The teacher had a wedding ring on her finger. I wondered how her husband felt about being the person she may love less than another but was able to live with. I was angry at this teacher for asking us to discuss people we love in a literature class.

*

In the basement, I played records. My favorite was *Nashville Skyline* by Bob Dylan. I listened over and over to a melancholy song called "I Threw It All Away," and I thought about Becky, about the inevitability of losing her, and I sat on the edge of my bed, leaning forward, my chest filling with misery in the basement.

*

Becky went to a college ninety minutes away from Peoria. Her mother taught me how to drive a stick shift in her driveway, which had a steep incline. She said, "If you can use a stick shift on a hill, you'll be able to use it anywhere." She loaned me her car to drive to Becky's college to visit her. As I drove, my head would begin to ache. When I got closer to campus, the headache would get worse. I took Tylenol three at a time. We would go out to eat and get a hotel room and make love. My head felt like it was imploding. I saw sparkles in the air, each a fuzzy image of a freshman college student, all the sparkles and images that would describe to Becky a picture of ease and fun and freedom that she of course would find far more desirable than the twistedness of me. I mean, who wouldn't?

*

Steve wrote on a piece of paper: "Route 474 is here now." He taped it to his wall. A new highway around Peoria had opened. Steve was celebrating. I imagined Steve writing the sign, making the letters laboriously, in his five-year-old's handwriting. I was happy for him, happy to witness this sign of his celebration.

*

A neighbor called and told me she had seen Steve on his bike on the Shade–Lohmann Bridge on Route 474, about ten miles from our home.

For some time, Steve's focus in life was the construction of the interstate highway bypass around Peoria, and the bridge being constructed on the bypass over the Illinois River. He loved interstate highways, and this was a new one. I understood, I thought. When a new album by a favorite musician or a new book by a favorite writer came out, I needed to have it instantly. The moment I first saw it was ecstasy.

I pictured Steve on his bike, riding on the interstate highway. It would have taken him a couple of hours just to get to the highway and along the highway to the bridge, and another couple of hours to get back. I pictured Steve, cars zipping around him, any one of which would kill him if he veered into its path, which was typical of his movements. I pictured Steve pumping the pedals on his bike, sweating, full of purpose.

I pictured Mom at home, in a fog, oblivious to the amount of time Steve had been gone.

I pictured Steve, pausing on the Shade–Lohmann Bridge, the object of his desire, looking around at whatever he needed to see—perhaps a sign, perhaps the texture of the pavement on the bridge, perhaps a mileage marker, perhaps a girder—with no expression on his face. I imagined myself on a bike, on that bridge, a feeling of calm and accomplishment. I felt proud of Steve, that he had constructed this adventure.

*

I heard a scraping sound when I pushed the brake pedal in my car, and Becky's stepfather, Chuck, offered to help me change the brake pads. He told me to pull the car into the loading dock of the beer-canning company where he worked. He was working second shift, and after five no trucks would be there. He said they didn't have any work just then and were all just sitting around smoking. When I arrived, he opened the loading dock door and motioned me to pull my car inside. The rest was rather a blur to me because I had no idea what he was doing with his various tools and parts. What I remember best is how he would pause every so often, step back, light a cigarette, scratch his red and gray beard, and smile, the beard folding up a bit as creases revealed themselves next to his eyes. I never felt more loved in my life than at that moment.

*

I invited Mom to go to a movie with Becky and me. We sat in this sequence: Mom, Becky, me. I wanted Mom to spend time with Becky. During the movie, Becky and I made a few whispered comments to one another. Mom moved to a seat across the aisle.

*

I called the psychiatrist—the family acquaintance I had sent Mom to see. We met in his lovely apartment in the north part of Peoria. We sat by a bay window. I talked for a few minutes. I told him that I was worried about Mom. I told him that I was worried about Steve, that Mom was having trouble taking care of him, that he was getting too old for his school program and I didn't know where he would go next. I told him that I felt bad all the time.

When I stopped, the doctor stared at me but didn't speak. Then he smiled a little crookedly.

He said, "You are a con man."

He said more things about me that I barely heard.

When he finished listing my crimes, he said, "Well, you've heard some things about yourself that you don't like, haven't you?"

I nodded and stood to leave.

*

Morning. Mom was in bed. She had a class to teach but was having trouble waking up.

The covers were down, and I could see that Mom's belly was distended. It seemed to have happened overnight. Her face was thin. Her arms were thinner than ever. But her belly was big, almost as if she were pregnant, but as if pregnancy were a disease.

She asked for aspirin. The bottle was on her bedside table. I shook out two and handed them to her, still lying on her back. She asked for water. Next to her bed was a glass half-full of orange juice and, I could smell, gin. The edges were crusty.

I said, "There's orange juice here. You can drink that."

She asked again for water. She struggled to sit up.

I said, "You can just use the orange juice."

I wanted her to know that I knew that there was gin in that glass. I wanted to see her drink it. She put the aspirin in her mouth, leaned toward the nightstand, took the glass from me. She let a bit of the gin and orange juice into her mouth, swallowed, gagged, and fell back onto the bed.

I went to the bathroom to get her a glass of water.

*

In the middle of an argument—they seemed to happen daily now—Mom told me that she wanted me to move out. I asked Becky's mom and stepdad if I could stay with them. Her mom turned to her husband, "We aren't going to let this nice boy live on the streets, are we?"

A few days later, Becky and I got a basement apartment two blocks from Mom's house.

Paul had already moved out.

I pictured Steve running around the house and Mom in bed.

*

I got a call from the arts center where Mom taught. The woman on the phone said that starting now, Mom would not be teaching there anymore, that she had missed too many classes. I visited Mom and, my voice soft, told her about the call. She was in bed. She said she didn't feel well.

I asked if Steve could stay with me while she was sick.

She nodded.

Now Mom was alone, the way, I believed, she had always intended to be.

*

I got Steve settled into our tiny apartment. He would sleep on the couch. We ate at his favorite restaurant that night—McDonald's. He loved McDonald's because the restaurants were all the same but still slightly different. Like school buses. Like episodes of *Sesame Street*.

That night, after Steve was tucked in, I sat on the edge of the couch and asked him if he wanted to talk about anything.

After a while, he said, "I'm living at your apartment."

I said, yes.

He said, "You have two sinks in your kitchen."

*

Steve stopped running. He adopted a walk that appeared to be the stride of someone rethinking the process of walking with each step. Or perhaps like a child trying to avoid stepping on sidewalk cracks to avoid breaking Mother's back.

*

Becky's mom smoked a brand of cigarette called Merit. Merit 100s, to be exact. The pack featured three thick diagonal stripes. The stripe on the right was yellow. The stripe in the middle was a dusty orange. The stripe on the left was darker greenish orange.

At the kitchen table in Becky's mom's house, I pointed to the middle stripe of the cigarette pack. I said to Becky's mom,

"That's the color of the whites of Mom's eyes."

She opened and closed her mouth. She said, "That's the color of the final stages of liver disease."

*

I went home. Mom was in bed. I told her I was worried. I told her that she needed to go to the doctor or to the hospital. She moaned and said no. I persisted. No.

I called the man who had been Mom's doctor since she came to Peoria. He had delivered us three boys and Steve's dead twin. His wife was a painter whom my parents respected and who admired my parents' work.

The doctor came and climbed the stairs to Mom's bedroom. I watched from the foot of the bed. The room was dark except for strips of light sneaking around the blinds. He bent over Mom. He looked at her eyes. He asked how she was feeling.

She told him that she wasn't feeling very well.

He told her she needed to go to the hospital now.

She began to rise from her bed.

*

Mom's father arrived. Steve and I met him at the airport. I drove—carefully so he wouldn't have anything to criticize—to the hotel where I had reserved a room for him. Steve asked to go up to the room so he could see the shape of the toilet, and whether it had a tank, like the one at our house, or a pipe connected directly to the wall, like the one in Grandma and Grandpa's apartment in Brooklyn.

*

In the hospital, from her bed, Mom said she had to get lunch for Steve.

I told her that Steve, who was in the hospital cafeteria, was fine.

She asked me to take the socks out of the refrigerator.

The nurse said that last night she had strapped Mom's arms to the bed because she was trying to get away.

*

Night. Paul and I sat with Steve in the waiting area near Mom's room.

We needed, we decided, to do something.

Paul and I talked to a nurse. We asked her, "What are you going to do?" We meant what was the nurse going to do now. What was happening to our mom?

The nurse said there wasn't much they could do.

We asked if she was going to die.

The nurse paged Mom's doctor. The nurse said he was still in the hospital at a meeting. He arrived with another doctor, who had been attending Mom. We stood away from Steve, who thank goodness was sitting, looking at a foldout map of Illinois highways.

"What are you going to do?" we asked.

"Well, she has very advanced liver disease."

"And…?"

"Well, the body needs a liver."

Paul asked if there was such a thing as a liver transplant. I scoffed even though I didn't know.

The doctors said that there comes a moment when the family realizes the patient isn't going to make it.

I felt stupid. I should have understood this before now. I shouldn't have panicked in front of these doctors.

*

Morning. Mom's hospital room. Huge bruises appeared on both her cheeks, chin, and surrounding one eye. Bruises on both arms. Strapped to the bed. She lifted her head and grinned at me. A grin of pure madness. Of resignation to madness. Of wallowing in madness. Of a new creature that had taken over my mom and flung her against her bed rails and against the wall and enjoyed doing it and wanted me to know it had enjoyed doing it and that it would do it again.

The face I had always known I would see.

The next morning, Grandpa and I walked from the parking deck into the hospital corridors. As we reached for the door of Mom's room, a nurse ran up and positioned herself between us and the door.

*

Steve sat on the couch in our basement apartment. I sat next to him, which meant that Steve was looking not at me but straight ahead toward the bookshelves against the opposite wall.

I was used to speaking to his profile, or to the back of his head.

"You know that Mom has been sick," I said.

"Mom has been sick?"

"Yes, Mom has been sick. And Mom's sickness got worse."

"Mom's sickness got worse?"

"Yes, Mom's sickness got worse. And today, Mom got so sick that she died."

A big smile broke out on Steve's face. He quickly covered it with his hand.

"Mom died?"

"Yes, Mom died."

"Mom died because she got sick."

"Yes."

"Dad died because he got a heart attack."

"Yes."

I gave Steve a hug. He didn't hug back.

I asked, "How do you feel about this?"

He said, "I feel sad." He paused.

I said, "What else?"

He said, "Who will take me to Summer Park Program?"

1980-1982

Before the memorial service, Mom's father looked over the three of us boys. I had bought Steve a suit at a department store a few days before. It was navy blue. My suit was a sort of dirty golden tan with a little texture to it. I had bought it at my new job—marking suits for alteration at a discount clothing outlet. I liked it; it made me feel confident. Paul wore one of Dad's sportscoats and ties, which I thought was a beautiful thing to do.

Grandpa Ray scanned the three of us. He said, "I see that Steven is the only one wearing a suit traditional for the occasion."

This time, at the service, I read a passage from an obscure novel called *Anaconda*, written by Jerry Bumpus when he was a graduate writing student at the University of Iowa. The novel is about a man who wanders around, homeless, sleeping where he can, often in the woods. Occasionally the man meets people. He has money, quite a bit of money, some of which he keeps in a belt around his waist, and that allows him to sit in bars and drink and sometimes talk with people. A romantic notion, for sure. Romantic to me, anyway. But at the end of the novel, the man dies alone. Before he dies, he confronts his solitude and the choices in his life that created the defeat of solitude, the defeat of dying alone. That's the passage I read. I wanted to shame Mom publicly. I wanted to yell at her publicly. I wanted to tell her how ridiculous and unnecessary it was for her to live her life alone and to die alone, and how cruel to inflict her self-immolation on the rest of us.

After the ceremony, as people left the nave and started to clog the assembly area, as I was keeping one eye on Steve while playing affable host (I could see people watching me and knew they were thinking, "didn't this kid's mom just die?"), Becky started crying. I asked what was wrong and touched her arm. She shook her head and shook my hand off her arm and ran into the bathroom.

I went to the door of the bathroom and called her name, but heard no response.

Still keeping Steve in sight, I scanned the area for an ally and saw the wife of a friend of Paul's. Her expression suggested she had seen the episode. She approached and volunteered to find out what was wrong.

I stayed near the door, shifting my weight from one foot to the other, trying to hide any panic on my face from departing guests, all the while ready to grab Steve if he made a run for the door or onto the altar.

When Paul's friend emerged from the bathroom, she was alone.

Becky, she said, was upset. She paused but she needn't have for my sake. I knew what was coming next, or at least I knew that I had done something wrong.

About that, I was right. The friend reported that Becky told her I had been closed off, I had been cold, I had been frozen.

Eventually the bathroom door opened, and Becky came out. I apologized. I did not know whether she would go home with me. I thought it likely she would not. She nodded, shoulders down, defeated. With Steve, we went back to our basement apartment.

*

Boy, I told myself, was I good at taking care of business. No one better than me at taking care of business, no matter how distasteful the business. In fact, the more distasteful the better.

I got the death certificate.

I worked with the executor to organize and dispose of house contents.

With Paul, I divided all the paintings in the house and garage and put them in storage.

I moved Becky, Steve, and myself into a nicer, two-bedroom apartment.

*

At the funeral, I had halfway expected some official personage to swoop in and take Steve away from me. I wasn't yet twenty-one. He was a minor. He was developmentally disabled. He would soon need to transition from classroom education to…to something. He would need a place to live—or would he live with me forever?

I asked one of Steve's teachers for advice. He suggested a residential facility nearby. I mentioned this facility to another of Steve's teachers. She said, "Oh, no. Steve would be valedictorian there."

I asked the executor about Steve's guardianship. I pointed out that the will named me as guardian, but that I wasn't even twenty-one. He said, as if I had distracted him from something important, "Mmmm?"

In order for Steve to get Social Security benefits, he had to be officially declared disabled. The Social Security office had Steve interviewed by a psychiatrist. A week later, I got a letter from Social Security denying us benefits and saying Steve was normal.

I said to someone, "I'm glad Mom is dead because this would have killed her."

I assembled a stack of papers a foot tall—reports refuting the finding—and filed an appeal.

*

Steve was a mimic. Confounded by the infinite choices available to him in each moment—for intonation, word choice, gesture—he found the easiest way to exist was to copy the example immediately in front of him (or, I supposed, to separate himself entirely from any examples, as I pictured him doing, with bliss and relief, on every bike ride, during every moment alone in his room).

With the tool of Steve's mimicry in hand, I went to work.

More than ever, I routinized our conversations, I slowed my speaking, I exaggerated emphasis on certain words, I modeled a best boy's musically polite voice.

I said, "Please pass the catsup." Lyrically, pleasantly.

He passed the catsup.

I said, "Thank you!"

He said, "Please pass the catsup."

I passed it, saying, "There you are!"

He said, "Thank you!"

When I dropped him off at his summer park program, I said, "Have a great day, Steve!"

He said, "Have a great day, Rob!"

At night, sitting on the edge of his bed, I said, "I love you, Steve."

He said, "I love you, Rob."

We were two best boys.

*

I had a belief. I held it close to me. That belief was that I had killed my mother.

The evidence was plentiful. I doubted that even Perry Mason could get me acquitted, had I wanted him to.

I had never liked my mother—really, ever.

I once poisoned her—presumably accidentally, but maybe not?

I was a con man, so how could anyone trust that I had good intentions in anything?

I could have insisted that Mom continue seeing the psychiatrist instead of giving up—that is, instead of me giving up—after she went to that one appointment.

I could have stopped her from drinking.

I could have noticed the physical signs of illness earlier and gotten her to a doctor sooner.

I could have given her a hug and told her that she wasn't alone, that I loved her.

I had no feelings, in general. I was the frozen man, just ask Becky, and wasn't that just the kind of person who would kill his mother?

*

Becky's parents were sitting in their kitchen as I entered. They didn't look up. They were side by side, looking toward the wall.

I asked what was wrong.

They said they had to take their dog to the vet to be put to sleep.

I said, "I could do that for you."

*

In bed one night, Becky woke me up. She said, "I hear a baby crying."

I listened.

She said, "It's saying, 'Mommy, let me out.'"

I listened. I heard the sound. It resembled a baby crying, maybe words. It went on and on. It sounded desperate.

She said, "We need to help."

I called the police. When they came to our door, I said, "My wife says she hears a baby saying, 'Mommy, let me out.'"

They went off to investigate. They came back and knocked on our door. One said, "We found some cats howling under your window." He smiled.

Becky, I thought, was not happy.

*

I kept a photograph of Becky and me in my top dresser drawer, in the back, in a corner. It was taken by Becky's mother.

Becky and I are in a park. The day is sunny. My arm is around Becky. I am looking at her. My expression is full of love, of awe in her existence, of solicitude. I appear to be asking her what I can do for her, how I can make her happy. She is smiling. Her face is bright. Her expression is carefree. She is not looking at me. She is not looking at the camera. She is looking away. Light light light. As if she does not know I am there. Light light light. As though any little thing, anything of modest interest, anything of momentary attraction, would cause her to float away, toward that thing. As though it could happen, would happen, at any moment. She looks so happy to be so light light light. Or perhaps incapable of being happy, just always feeling light light light.

*

I went to work at a farm-supply warehouse near the river. The other workers sometimes showed up and sometimes didn't. And sometimes showed up and were sent home because they were drunk.

A man who was from Vietnam and spoke no English picked parts from rows of bins to fill orders. I imagined he was fifty but he looked far more frail than that.

When he was hired, I saw a woman I assumed was his wife come into the warehouse with him. She spoke to the manager. She spoke minimal English, but more than he did. He was shorter than she was. He looked on as she spoke, his lips showing a confused-seeming smile.

The manager told us his name was Linh, and he wrote his name in large, shaky characters at the bottom of each packing slip.

When he didn't have any orders to pick, he sat on a folding chair at the head of one of the rows of parts bins. He crossed his legs and smoked.

I noticed at some point that he no longer smoked. He looked lost, sitting there, on that naked folding chair, with his legs crossed, looking at the wall over the packing table.

I mentioned to the manager that Linh seemed to have stopped smoking. The manager told me that his wife stopped letting him buy cigarettes. I wondered how the manager had that information but trusted it.

One day, during lunch break, Linh went into the tiny office and came out with a piece of typing paper. I sat at the packing table, eating my lunch, and watched him. He tore the paper widthwise in thirds. He took one of the strips of paper and formed what looked like a narrow funnel. Holding the funnel together with one hand, he reached with his other hand into his brown-paper lunch bag and withdrew a pouch of pipe tobacco, the kind they sold for fifty cents at the drug store. With one hand, he opened the flap of the pouch and withdrew a clump of tobacco, which he carefully dropped into the funnel. He tightened the funnel a bit, stood, and approached me. He held out the homemade cigarette, smiled, and lightly waved it toward me.

I held up a finger, meaning, "Wait," went into the warehouse area, and returned with a book of matches. He nodded, sat back down, and lit his cigarette, which flamed a bit at its seams. He crossed his legs and smoked.

During the afternoon, I stole two cigarettes from someone's pack sitting on a stool, and during the afternoon break, I gave them to Linh. He smiled and nodded several times.

*

I wrote a letter to mom's father and his wife. Just the usual. News from the family. Steve's school activities. Paul's music activities. My school and work. I used the same salutation I had used for every letter I ever wrote to him and to his wife: "Dear Grandpa Ray and Grandma Dorothy." We kids called mom's mother Grandma Julie, and we called Grandpa Ray's second wife Grandma Dorothy. We didn't make that up ourselves. I assumed that Mom told us to use those names. I mean, where else would we have come up with that formulation?

I received a letter from Grandpa Ray. It started: "Dear Robert, Thank you for your letter. You are to address your grandmother as Grandma Ray, not as 'Grandma Dorothy.' There is only one Grandma Ray." He wanted to obliterate his first wife, my other grandma, from my consciousness. I flung the letter away from me as if it were burning my fingers. Even as I was recoiling from the letter I was reminded of my dad's mom flinging the phone receiver away when she heard her son was dead. Only that time, the cause was not her fault. She was experiencing horror. In this case, I had caused my horror.

*

Steve sat beside me, in front of the television. I heard him whisper something to himself. Then he smiled and started to laugh quietly.

I asked what was funny. I said I wanted to know, I wanted to laugh too.

He said loudly, "I don't know."

I asked again.

He said, "I don't know!"—louder this time.

*

In the morning, I played three games of solitaire before making coffee. I played more solitaire while drinking coffee. I played solitaire while eating lunch. I played solitaire after dinner while watching a baseball game on TV. At first, I kept track in my mind of the number of matches I won but soon gave up. Playing solitaire was like listening to white noise to drown out the distracting sounds of your thoughts.

*

"I was trying to tell him that he should clean his room, but he walked by me like I wasn't even there. What an arrogant bastard."

I awkwardly tried to give Becky a hug. "You'll get used to him."

"But it's been more than a year."

"Well, that's not really so long. You'll get used to him."

"But don't you know what I mean?"

"Yes, I guess I know. I guess you're right. He is that way."

*

Becky and I were sitting in a small classroom. Putty-color folding chairs with tablet arms were scattered around the room, more or less facing a screen on one wall. Two of the four rows of fluorescent lights were off, and photographs of paintings appeared on the screen slowly, one by one. Study session for modern-art history class.

I loved this class. The professor told me that many of the slides used in the class were taken by my father. "The paintings I didn't like, but he did," the professor, who painted huge faces of beautiful young men, said to me after the first day of class.

I spent hours, days, years with my parents in museums and galleries looking at these paintings and sculptures, but Dad and Mom never said anything about the work. Occasionally a few words to each other, but almost nothing to me. I could, however, sense Dad's joy from time to time—for example, Duane Hanson's realistic, life-sized sculptures of tourists and Bruce Nauman's fifteen-foot-high glowing corridors. Dad and I enjoyed them together. It was like playing a wordless, slow-motion game of tag.

In class, in the dark, notebook on my desk, watching the

artwork on the screen, listening to the professor say the names of the artists, placing them in chronology, hearing a few words about their lives and the features of their work, was as magical as caulk floating down from the sky and settling into the gaps between tiles.

Also, my last name was Fromberg. If there was one place where that name had a legacy, it was in this building. And I didn't want to screw it up. On my first quiz, I had one point taken off. The next one I scored 100%. I planned to continue that.

The professor was not at this study session, just a teacher's assistant. I assumed that she was just a few years older than I was, but she seemed impossibly mature, impossibly beautiful. Yet, I thought, maybe I was a rival for maturity, sitting here with Becky, who was practically my wife, someone with whom I spent most days in classes, someone with whom I ate and slept. I felt like a person of stature.

As the slides progressed, the students chatted with one another in a way they never would have if the professor were in the room. I studied each slide carefully. These were the slides that would be on the midterm test. We had a list of the titles and artists. I was taking notes furiously, describing in my notes the appearance of each painting, sometimes attempting a crude drawing. The teacher's assistant advanced the slides.

Chatting was not really the right word. My dad would have called it kibitzing. But that wasn't the right word either. They were joking about the images on the slides. They were sliding their desks around. They were snickering, giggling, laughing.

I continued to take notes, but I had trouble paying attention.

My face felt hot. I glanced at Becky. She was looking at the screen, her face placid.

With each remark, each grunt or giggle, my face felt hotter. My arms began to vibrate. My writing was becoming illegible.

The sounds were coming from everyone, it seemed, from every desk in the small room, except for mine and Becky's. The others all seemed to know each other, although that was unlikely. Yet they shared a language. And a sense of impropriety. A disrespect for the art, for the teacher, for the teacher's assistant. They disrespected me. They disrespected my father. They disrespect my desire to absorb this material, my desire to get a perfect score on the midterm.

They were the center of the universe. I was hovering outside.

My head filled and then emptied. Each sound was like an electric shock. At the next sound I stood, catching my arm on the desk and toppling it and my notebook.

I screamed words that I did not control. I said "shut up" and I said "respect" and I said other words that I was able to enunciate but that seemed to orbit my head.

The room was silent. I righted my chair, picked up my notebook, and sat.

The silence was more painful than the noise had been. The teacher's assistant asked to see me in the hall outside the room. She exited first. I followed. Becky accompanied me.

She told me that my outburst was not appropriate, that I should have told her if I had a problem. I looked at her brown leather boots. Occasionally I glanced at her face, its annoyance, the annoyance of dealing with a child.

We reentered the room, and the assistant resumed advancing

slides, and I had what I had wanted, but didn't want now: silence.

As Becky and I walked home, I said, "That assistant should have stopped them from talking before I said anything." But my memory of the assistant's expression, of well-considered annoyance, told me I was the one who had been in the wrong. I wondered how soon Becky would realize she was living with such a child.

*

I sat on the edge of Steve's bed before I turned out his lights. I waited for him to speak.

"My dad is dead," he said. "My mom is dead. My grandpa is dead. My grandma is dead."

"It's sad," I said.

"It's sad," he said.

*

In the Peoria Public Library, in a directory of services for the developmentally disabled across the country, under Illinois, I found a place north of Chicago. Residential. Vocational. It didn't mention autism, but it sounded OK. I called, asked a few questions, and made an appointment. Steve, Becky, and I drove to Chicago. I got a speeding ticket along the way.

The facility was off the highway, visible down a hill like some kind of fairgrounds. It was a working farm. It was not part of any city or town. We pulled into the driveway, parked, and got a tour.

It had gift shops and a restaurant. It had people who were blind and mentally challenged and maybe, the tour guide said, two people with autism. The residents lived in a dorm and in apartments. They worked on the farm and in the shops. People visited the farm and the gift shops on weekends. The visitors must have liked to see the disabled people being so productive and behaving just like normal people, but, you know, kind of cute imitations of normal people, and liked to see the disabled people they were giving their money to.

The staff showed Steve the place where he might live and where he might work.

They asked him what he thought.

He said, "Good."

I said things like, "You could work here; how about that?" in an upbeat voice.

He said, "Good," in a tone that matched mine.

I kept looking up the hill at the interstate highway. I saw Steve making a break for it the moment he got a chance. I thought of him standing on the highway looking at signs.

At home, several days later, Becky asked me when I was going to fill out the application. I slammed a cup on the coffee table. The cup broke. Becky had gotten it for me as a Valentine's Day present. Becky cried. Then we cleaned the apartment together.

I filled out lots of forms and copied lots of reports. I took Steve to the doctor for a physical exam. I sent everything in. Four weeks later, I got a letter saying Steve was accepted and that he was number six on their waiting list.

Well, that sounded good. But also, I kept thinking about Steve walking up that hill and standing on the side of the highway. I thought he might like that, if that was all he could do. It was something.

In the following months, I would occasionally say something upbeat about the place, and Steve would say, in my tone, "Good." But he didn't raise his eyebrows, which is what he did when he said the words like "glass elevator" or "Peoria airport."

Six months later, I called the facility. I said hi. I said my brother had been accepted six months ago. I said at the time he had been number six on the waiting list. I asked when, roughly, he might expect to get in. The lady on the phone said, oh, the turnover was maybe one every year or two, so it would be a while.

That was fine. Fuck them. Back to the library.

*

I had wide, pointy shoulders. Also, I was skinny as hell—size twenty-seven waist. Picture a skeleton on a wire hanger.

So buying a shirt that fit was a problem. But fit was only the second problem. The first problem was, well, shirts.

In Peoria, there were two kinds of shirts. One kind was casual. These shirts had patterns. Windowpane checks. Broad stripes. And they had colors—greens and blues and yellows and reds in various combinations. That was no good. I could not wear shirts with patterns or noticeable colors. People would look at me and, if not laugh in my face, turn and snicker or shake their heads in pity. Especially people my age.

Sometimes I would see a plain-looking, casual shirt hanging on a rack. But on closer inspection, there would be something: a logo on the front or, more often than you might imagine, a huge picture on the back of a cartoon motorcycle, a galloping horse, and, once, a chainsaw.

Which left me with dress shirts. That was fine. I thought I could wear a plain dress shirt with a pair of jeans, and I would be suitably nondescript.

Of course, there were many stripes and checks to be avoided among dress shirts, but there were also plain shirts guaranteed not to have pictures of chainsaws on them. Of course, I had to take that on faith, because dress shirts never hung on hangers. They came folded in clear plastic. So I couldn't see the full shirts. And I couldn't try them on.

At a department store at the mall, Becky at my side, while Steve was in school, I bought a cream-colored shirt. At home, I tried it on. The seams sat on the edges of my shoulders all right, but the shirt hung on me like a garbage sack. I could kind of gather all the excess fabric and tuck it in and more or less manage that problem, but another problem proved fatal: From the shoulders, the fabric pulled badly toward the top buttons on the placket, creating ridiculous gutters of fabric. Still, I tried wearing the shirt around the house. The gutters became hideous diagonal creases.

When I lived in New York, clothing was simple. I dressed more or less like The Ramones—t-shirt, jeans, and a leather jacket. But now, in Peoria, it seemed to me that this was not an option. Not with a live-in girlfriend. Not with a brother to take care of. Not in college. Not while maintaining my anonymity.

A few days later, Becky and I went back to the store, and I chose a shirt a half-size larger than the one I had bought. Maybe, I thought, a larger size would eliminate the pulling at the shoulders. I explained my problem to the man at the counter. I held out the plastic-packaged shirt and asked whether I could unwrap the shirt and try it on. He did not respond. The shirt seemed to hover between us. I said I would probably buy the shirt, but I would feel better if I could try it on. Without speaking, he took the shirt package from me and began unwrapping. The process seemed endless—clear plastic cover, pins everywhere, cardboard under the collar, cardboard and tissue inside the folded fabric. He handed me the shirt.

In the dressing room, decidedly alone, I took off my shirt, hung it on the hook, and tried on this new shirt. The cuffs hung to my thumbs, but sleeves can be rolled up. I buttoned the shirt. The fabric around my body was more voluminous than the other shirt. Oddly, although the shoulder seams gave my shoulders a bit more room, the diagonal gutters from shoulder to buttons were deeper.

One way or another, I was doomed. A larger shirt than the last one was worse. But somehow, a smaller shirt than the last one, with even less shoulder room, would inevitably also be worse.

That consideration quickly was covered by another realization: I could not buy this shirt. I would have to face the salesman.

I took off the new shirt, put on my old shirt, and considered folding the new one to resemble how it had looked in the package. I pictured myself working on this for an hour. And without the various pieces of carboard and pins, the result would be a pathetic replica of the original crisp presentation.

I left the dressing room and laid the shirt on the counter in front of the salesman. Open, the shirt seemed to catch the air and float down. What could I do? I said, "I'm sorry, it doesn't fit." He snorted, snatched up the shirt, and stared at it, appearing to be more lost than angry. I touched Becky's shoulder. She looked like she had lost a war. We left.

*

Steve had a frequent movement while walking—a kind of sway. Maybe it was more like a basketball player, standing still, looking for someone to pass the ball to. Steve would be walking fairly quickly, looking at something to his left, say, and he would go slightly past the thing he was looking at, then, feet planted and looking squarely toward that thing, he would sway his upper body back and forth, as if trying to get the perfect angle, or rapidly comparing ever-so-slightly different angles. Sometimes he would sway four or five times, each time seeming just about to walk on, but stopping and jerking back to renew his view.

When he went out for walks, I would watch him through our window, on the sidewalk, doing his back-and-forth sway, his eyes on the house next door. I rather enjoyed his focus. I imagined the beautifully subtle differences in what he saw from such slight shifts in perspective.

Sometimes, after Steve had been out for a few minutes on a walk or bike ride, the door buzzer would sound, and at the outer door of the apartment I would be met with Steve and a police officer on either side of him. The police would begin their explanation of the situation, while Steve accompanied their recitation with "Well…well…well…well." Once a neighbor, watching from her front window, saw Steve looking at her house and lurching back and forth. Another time, officers in a police car saw Steve on his bike darting away from our apartment building's garages, chased him, and stopped him.

When I saw the police officers, I knew that they saw in Steve what I saw: the unusual intensity, bordering on panic, in his expression. Couldn't that expression be of a person who was pondering a home invasion or fleeing from a break-in? I knew that Steve was just looking for something wonderful, like the new sign on Elmwood Street, but how would the police know.

No hard feelings.

*

In the grocery store parking lot, a man approached me. "There's no place in this town where I can get my Schwinn bike fixed."

"No?"

"Not a one," he said. "You'd think there would be some place, even in Peoria."

We walked together down the row of cars.

I said, "What about that place on Sheridan?"

"No," he said, "that place closed down. Now it's a rug shop."

By then we were at my car. I got my keys out of my pocket. He kept walking. We didn't say anything more. I wanted to tell him that it had been nice talking with him.

*

I found a paper written by my mother in impeccable cursive, dated February 12, 1943, for "Language 8B." Mom would have been twelve years old.

My Father

His face is slightly wrinkled not by age but from study, yet there are signs of gray appearing around his temples. He is a happy easygoing man content with life. Living it for what it is. Not looking ahead for a better life for as he says, "There is no better." His mind is keen and alert. When he reads he saps every bit of information from his reading be it a novel or history book, of which he prefers the latter.

My mom, even at age twelve, understood what Grandpa Ray did and did not mean by "There is no better." From Grandpa Ray's perspective, "There is no better" did not mean, "These are the best times, so enjoy them." What he did mean, I was certain, was that to imagine happiness could exist was futile, perhaps infantile.

*

One of the professors I respected most at the university taught Spanish. She was fairly young—perhaps mid-forties—and was decisive, thoughtful, warm. I told her that I was living with someone, that we would marry. She said, "No, don't marry a Peoria girl."

*

I kept the school lunch menus taped to the wall in the living room near my desk. Each week, Steve and I reviewed the menus, and we marked the days he would eat the lunch being served and which days I would pack him a lunch.

One day, I received a call from Steve's teacher. Because Steve had misbehaved in school, he had not been allowed to have the cookie served at lunch.

That evening, I sat in the living room reading. From my peripheral vision, I saw movement in the hallway that led from the bedrooms to the living room. Steve was moving slowly. I pretended not to watch. With tiny footsteps, he made his way down the hallway. He was holding something in his right hand. Finally, he emerged from the hallway, moved quickly to the wall where the lunch menus were posted, leaned over, made a quick motion of some sort, and exited back down the hall.

I rose and walked to the sheet of menus, leaned over, and looked at it.

Steve had crossed out "cookie" on that day's menu.

I thought about the satisfaction Steve felt crossing off that word, the restoration of the rightness of things.

I imagined myself taking a piece of typing paper from a drawer in my desk. I imagined which words I would list on the paper and which, once I had written them, I would cross out.

*

I told the school that Steve needed some kind of vocational training. He was, after all, now seventeen, and I assumed that he wouldn't be in school much longer.

This was a pitfall of Steve's education in Peoria. My parents had essentially blackmailed the school district into setting up the program. That meant that Steve was the oldest person in the program. And that meant that there was no path for anyone older than he was.

Steve began working half days, three days a week, at the Goodwill thrift store. I went there to help him with any rough spots as he made the transition.

Steve's supervisor was a young guy in a wheelchair. He had been paralyzed in a motorcycle accident. He propelled himself crisply around the crowded aisles of the store.

Steve's job was mostly sweeping. I didn't understand how there would be four hours' worth of sweeping, but I didn't say anything.

Steve didn't have good fine-motor coordination, and sweeping in corners was a struggle. The supervisor mostly zoomed around and told stories about riding motorcycles. My parents had thought that, with his skill for making maps and diagrams, Steve might become an architect.

*

The letter began, "Dear Robert, We read your letter and were moved by your situation. Let me tell you about our resources in North Carolina, and we can talk further about what options you might want to pursue."

When I had finished the letter, I went back to the beginning: "Dear Robert, We read your letter and were moved by your situation. Let me tell you about our resources in North Carolina."

I read it again: "Dear Robert, We read your letter and were moved by your situation."

Our situation. Someone had learned about our situation. Someone was moved by the situation. Someone was moved by what I had done.

*

I told Steve that North Carolina had good weather and lots of new highways.

He replied, "North Carolina has good weather and lots of new highways?"

I said, "Yes," putting a lift in my voice. "How does that sound?"

He said, with no lift, "A little good."

1981-1985

When my grandparents in Brooklyn died, and the older of the two downstairs aunts died, my Aunt Mary was the only one left in that house.

By then, my dad's sister, Aunt Norma, and her husband, Uncle Jerry, had retired and moved from Long Island to Florida. Shortly after that, Aunt Norma died of lung cancer. One of her sons said to me, "My mom never smoked a cigarette in her life." But I remembered seeing cigarettes and an ashtray in her house.

Uncle Jerry found a retirement home in Florida for Aunt Mary. He told me that when Aunt Mary got to Florida, after a lifetime in Brooklyn, she said, "It's like waking up in heaven."

When Steve, Becky, and I visited North Carolina, it was like waking up in heaven.

I asked the head of the autism agency which city in North Carolina had the best services for Steve. He refused to answer.

He asked which city we liked the best, not for Steve but for ourselves.

I looked at Becky. She nodded. I turned back to the man. I said shyly, "Well, we like Chapel Hill."

He said, "Fine."

We worked out a plan for Steve. For continuity, he would go to school for one more year in a class for autistic people at a junior high school in town. He would, "because of your situation," be one of the first people to move into a group home opening within several months. After Steve's year in school, he would go to a vocational workshop. Steve could work there indefinitely, or the agency's program for supervised employment could get him a job. He would attend social skills classes, be assigned a "best buddy" for social outings, and play on sports teams. "But," the man said, "if a person wants to sit and spin a pencil for several hours, that's fine too."

I assured Steve that we would visit Peoria at least once each year.

*

I wrote stories about taking walks with my wife, surrounded by grass and shrubs and trees of super-saturated green and feeling the warm breeze.

Steve rapidly assembled a deep knowledge of the streets of Chapel Hill and the routes to nearby cities like Durham and Raleigh.

The autism program even helped us find a babysitter, a blind young man. One night, Becky and I left Steve with the babysitter, went to the police station—a lovely new building—and got married in a tiny conference room while three employees pointed and smiled through the small window in the door. On the way home, we stopped at a grocery store and got a frozen, white Sara Lee cake.

I stumbled on a record by Tommy Dorsey, and the lush opening of the song "Imagination" reminded me of the music I heard on television shows in my grandparents' and aunts' homes in Brooklyn. I listened to the record over and over.

Steve moved into the brand-new group home. His managers were just a bit older than me. They reminded me of the students of my dad's, who watched us on the rare occasions when Mom and Dad went out. Steve's housemates were each dazzlingly uninhibited. Steve said, "It looks new."

I said, "What does it remind you of?"

He said, "Our old apartment on High Street in Peoria."

I said, "What else do you notice about it?"

He said, "It has a gas stove. It has two tubs in the sink. It has six bedrooms. It has three bathrooms. The toilet has a tank."

I said, "Are you ready to move here?"

He said, "I want to live with you and visit Peoria."

I said, "You'll be taking a new bus to school."

He said, "Yes." His eyebrows rose. His voice picked up some energy. "I'll be taking a new bus to school!"

The night Steve moved, I lay in bed and tried to figure out how I felt, but I couldn't. I asked myself what this feeling reminded me of. It reminded me of the feeling after Mom's funeral. That feeling was blank.

I attended graduate school in the mountains of North Carolina—what was called a low-residency program, meaning I was on campus for two weeks in the summer and two weeks in the winter, but otherwise at home. It was a Master of Fine Arts in writing program, designed largely for adults, people who have families to attend to, jobs. Well-respected authors taught there. I was the youngest student. I didn't find the work too challenging—writing fiction, reading and writing reactions to published fiction. Still, when I was on campus and my work was being critiqued or I was speaking in class, I often felt that other students, and sometimes faculty, wanted to say something to me that they stopped just short of saying aloud.

I had plenty of time to take Steve for drives.

I had plenty of time to go for walks, go for drives with Becky. Just Becky and me. We could go to restaurants, just us, and I would order food just for myself, not needing to guide Steve's choice or to help him state his order to the server.

I wrote a poem about the freedom a couple felt when their infant child died—freedom to grocery shop unencumbered, to see a movie any time they wanted.

Sometimes I went out without Becky and without Steve. Those times, as I was about to open the apartment door upon my return, I would be pretty sure that Becky and all her belongings were gone.

*

I started playing solitaire again, sometimes for several hours a day.

I began to watch baseball on television—every night.

Becky took up photography.

On our walks, Becky and I often pointed at simple things, things not so common in Peoria—a lovely house, a particularly lush tree, a sweeping lawn—and say "look!" and "yes!"

After a while, having run out of obvious things to point to, I would still make the effort, perhaps with a long driveway or a cloud formation or a stone fence, but Becky's responses were less enthusiastic than before.

*

When we drove on the highway, Steve took pictures. I could not discern what specific objects he was taking pictures of. When he would raise the camera and I heard the click as he pushed the button, I didn't see a particular sign or a billboard or even something subtle like a mile marker.

I asked him, gently, as was necessary so he didn't get alarmed or annoyed when he had been concentrating or when there had been a period of silence, "Hey Steve, what did you just take a picture of?"

"I don't know."

"Was there something interesting on the highway?"

"I don't know."

When we got his pictures developed, I pulled them from the envelope and studied them. One after another, the photos showed a bland, blank road, sometimes a railing along the side, grass, sky. I could not see anything identifying. Yet, even as we sat in Steve's room at the group home, when Steve was looking at one of these undistinguished highway pictures, even if the picture was taken many years before, and I asked, "What highway is that?" he would say, "Route 70 near the Kittatinny Tunnel, Pennsylvania, March 1975."

I liked looking at Steve's pictures. They made me feel small and anonymous and comforted.

*

Every Sunday, I took Steve to lunch. He always chose a McDonald's, although not always the same McDonald's. Sometimes he spent the night with Becky and me, but not very often because I knew Becky did not like this, which I understood. Steve came to live with us almost as soon as Becky and I had moved in together. For Becky, I knew it was like getting married at age eighteen and immediately giving birth to a sixteen-year-old. Steve lived with us for—how long?—almost five years. Was that possible? I had taken away any normalcy in Becky's life.

I tried to talk with Steve, but it was difficult when we were driving because he was concentrating on the roads. It was also difficult to talk with him at McDonald's, because he was concentrating on his eating—which he did methodically, not leaving a crumb behind—and his surroundings. I did, however, have my reliable conversational standbys. When we went to the McDonald's in nearby Hillsborough, I would ask, "Steve, what does Hillsborough remind you of?"

He would reply, "It reminds me of the George Washington Parkway near Washington, DC. What does Hillsborough remind you of?"

I would say, "It reminds me of the George Washington Parkway, too. It also reminds me of Route 29 near Peoria."

His eyebrows up, he would reply, "Me too! It reminds me of Route 29 too!"

Before I would take Steve home, we would stop at a gas station and look at the shelves of candy.

"You can pick one," I would say.

He would look at the shelves for a minute or two, which I could tell disconcerted the clerk at the counter. I would tell other customers in line to step past us.

"It's hard," he would say. "There are so many choices."

I would say, "Can you think of three you want to choose from?"

He would immediately name one, then, his finger hovering over the options, name another, and then, after a longer period, name another.

"Well," I would say, "which of those three would you like today?" He usually chose the first one he named.

At this point, I needed to be very careful. It was critical that I not make any sound that could possibly be construed as anything other than full support for his choice. An accidental, "Hmm," or "Ah" would send Steve into, "I don't know! This is hard!" and I would need to slowly reassure him that his choice was a great one, and that he could get the others another time.

When I dropped Steve off at the group home, standing inside the front door, listening to the buzz of activity, I would hug Steve, but he would not hug back. When I would release the hug, he would slide his foot forward and touch the toe of his shoe to the toe of my shoe.

*

Becky and I were window shopping at a nearby mall, looking at sets of dishes, when a man beside us at the window pointed to one set and said to the woman at his side, "I can't stand that shade of blue."

As usual, I was astonished that people had opinions. That a person could see a movie, for example, or look at a painting, or read a news story about politics, or see a set of dishes, and immediately offer a judgment on that thing, even—or perhaps especially—something as clear as, "I like it."

When I was alone, I sometimes gingerly formulated such an opinion, but I knew that if I were with another person, I would wait for that person to opine first and shape my reaction to complement theirs, as I had done with my friend in New York who hated everything. When I did find myself having a strong personal opinion—for example, that I loved the green color of the outfield and the movement of a curveball that I saw in baseball games on television—I kept that opinion to myself, and I did not share the object of my opinion with anyone else, just in case they disagreed and my opinion would then need to vanish.

When we first started living together, Becky was the exception. With Becky, I could state opinions unreservedly, and my memories of those early drives to Chicago or North Carolina were full of my pronouncements, pronouncements I would not have dared to make to the guy who hated everything or to one of my classmates in college or graduate school. My memory told me that Becky responded favorably to my pronouncements, or at least not unfavorably. I would have noticed that.

Lately, however, when I stated an opinion, Becky responded by tightening her lips or tersely nodding, and I began waiting for her to speak first and to shape my responses to complement her observations.

*

Every Sunday at 8 PM I called Grandma Julie—my mother's mother—who now lived in a seedy residence hotel in downtown Seattle. She loved to talk about literature and writing. She said that whenever she watched Johnny Carson's show, she looked for my name among the writers. "Why," she asked, "don't you get a job writing for Johnny Carson?"

I spent evenings looking through bookstores for collections of short stories or essays she might like, in type large enough for her to see. Books with large type especially for people with trouble seeing were verboten, however. "I don't want any book like that," she would say.

*

Becky and I were out for dinner. I looked at my watch, held below the tabletop so Becky couldn't see it. 7:10. We had just ordered. I started to panic. The baseball game started at 7:35. We would never get home in time for me to see the beginning. How had I not managed the timing better? I needed to see the games from beginning to end. I needed to see the arc of events in its entirety. I needed to see the first moment of those glowing colors—the uniforms, the grass. I needed to see the gradual change in those colors as the sun disappeared and the stadium lights took over, the drama of those lights easily fighting off the surrounding darkness.

When the food arrived, I ate quickly, hoping Becky would follow my lead.

*

Mom's ashes were still in the brown-paper-wrapped box they were mailed in. I kept them on the upper shelf of my side of the closet. I thought that maybe, when I visited Grandma Julie in Seattle, I would pour them into Puget Sound. Sometimes I wondered what the box beneath the brown paper looked like. I imagined that her ashes were clumping together like sugar in a humid house.

*

Each night, Becky and I discussed where we wanted to go out to eat, choosing from among the four or five restaurants we typically visited, sometimes tossing a new possibility into the mix, just for discussion.

Most nights, we walked in the nearby shopping mall, enjoying the bright lights, observing the small changes.

I imagined we were an old couple living in a small town, with no expectation of a life any more exciting than this.

*

At school, during one of the residency periods in the mountains, a group of students were invited to a faculty member's house for dinner. After dinner, someone turned on a record player, and people started dancing.

I began to feel dizzy. I wondered how these people, who

had been chatting a few minutes before, could now be moving their bodies without inhibition, jumping, reaching toward the ceiling, and all this in a home of a faculty member, a home none of them had ever been to before. I wondered how these people, many of whom had met each other only a week before, could now spontaneously dance together.

At the end of one song, someone yelled, "Play it again," and the song started over, and the dancers jumped even higher, some of their outstretched hands touching the ceiling this time.

The woman with short dark hair was ten years older than I was. She told me she was married to a man who worked as a congressional staff person in Washington, D.C. He did not understand her love of writing, she told me. She wanted to have a baby, she told me. I loved the whitish circles under her eyes from the makeup that she used presumably to hide dark circles. They made her look tired and sad, and I loved to look at them.

She and I talked for a while, and then she was dancing. Everyone, it seemed, was dancing. Dizziness moved from my head to my eyes and my ears. Nausea rose toward my throat. My knees felt liquid. I put my hand on the back of a sofa, but by reducing my legs' responsibility for keeping me upright, I felt even less capable of standing, of remaining conscious to tolerate my shame and to not fall in love with the woman with short dark hair and whitish circles under her eyes.

My humiliation would be cemented if I left, but staying was no longer an option.

When I closed the front door, I was surrounded by darkness. Even the light from the house didn't penetrate the darkness. I remembered walking here, following a group of students, while it was still light. I remembered that the house was down a paved lane, thick woods on either side, no other houses around, although I could see none of that now. I took several steps forward. With each step, I put my foot forward and tapped the surface to determine if I was still on the pavement. I had no sense of what was straight ahead. I had no sense of the length of the lane or which way I would turn when I got to its end.

The dancing and the circles under the eyes of the sad woman ricocheted around my chest, and my eyes burned.

I felt my way to another lane and turned right. I saw faint lights in the distance that I assumed were the few buildings that constituted campus.

I began to run.

When I reached the one-story wood-frame dormitory, I went to the tiny room, with a door that opened to the outside, with a pay telephone.

My wife's voice came through the receiver.

"Tell me what you look like," I said. "I can't remember what you look like."

She began to cry.

*

I told the woman who covered the dark circles under her eyes with makeup that it was easier to have my parents dead than alive.

She told me I was a horrible person. She paused and said, "Not horrible, but…"

She didn't go on.

*

On the first Tuesday of each month, I visited the bookstore in the mall. A mass-market publisher was republishing one book each month in the *Nero Wolfe* mystery series. The books originally were published between 1934 and 1975. The first Tuesday of the month was when the newly republished title would appear on the bookstore shelf in our city. As I approached the shelf each month, I felt my excitement rising, and it would crest when I saw the unfamiliar spine of the new issue. Once in a while, the new title would not be there, and that was a disappointment, but also that would extend the excitement, the sense of purpose, and inevitably the book would be there the next day.

The books featured a consistent cast of characters, defined by consistent characteristics, in a consistent setting, facing similar challenges and resolutions from book to book. I had no interest in who committed the crime. I would forget the name of the culprit the moment I closed the book after reading the last page. I enjoyed the author's syntactic gymnastics and found sentence structures from the books appearing in my writing. Mostly, however, I read the books because they blocked thinking without requiring any emotional engagement. I read an interview with the author in which he said that he started out writing literary novels, but that writing good literature required having deep feelings, and he didn't have deep feelings.

Becky read the books too, and she and I would discuss the signals we found that offered subtle shadings to the traits of the characters. I read the books every night. I reread the books multiple times. I selected the four titles I would take with me to live in the single-room apartment or shack in the middle of nowhere or on the park bench where I would live when every other facet of my life dissolved, when nothing was left but bad feelings. Even then, these four books would block out those emotions until I died.

*

Becky and I moved, from one apartment complex in Chapel Hill to another apartment complex in Chapel Hill to an apartment complex in the town contiguous to Chapel Hill to a duplex town house in Raleigh.

In between moving, we talked about moving.

*

I got my Master of Fine Arts degree and published enough stories to be hired to teach one creative writing class per week at Duke University.

I got a job at a printing plant, proofreading the yellow pages of the telephone books for small towns throughout North Carolina.

Type was set by two men hunched over ancient keyboards of tall, beastly machines with swinging arms that spit out lead slugs with the letters keyed in by the men. One of the men was nearly blind. He said he did not want to be a burden to his family. A few months after I began working there, he shot himself in the face with a shotgun.

I worked in a small room with two women whom, within two days, I loved. Lida was in her thirties, with a long face, no makeup, dead-straight limp hair, a nimbus of confidence and many friends to talk with on the phone and to drink many drinks with every night. Lida was a cousin of Ava Gardner and told stories about spending time with her in rural North Carolina. Edna was a widow. Edna said, "The only man I want has one foot in the grave and the other foot on a banana peel." When a few rare flakes of snow began to fall, Edna would grab her coat and head for the door, announcing, "I can't drive in this mess." Edna said, whenever Lida left the room, "I love that little girl." When we were not sure how to spell a word on our long galley sheets, we discussed our beliefs as to the word's spelling rather than looking in the large hardcover dictionary that rested on each of our desks.

The boss entered our room once or twice each week, smiled, and said a few words so garbled as to be incomprehensible, while seeming to bounce his testicles through the pocket of his loose-fitting suit pants (or, as Lida said, "tumbling his prunes").

I learned how to spell "ophthalmology."

With one exception, it was a perfect job. That exception was the coffee. Coffee was a moment of joy. Coffee was a comfort. Coffee was calming. Coffee was one of my only good memories: coffee in stained porcelain cups for thirty-five cents at diners in New York, coffee in paper cups with pictures of the Parthenon from diners in New York where I had to beg the countermen not to include cream, the first pot of coffee made in a percolator on my first gas stove ever in my first apartment, the ways I explored how to make good coffee on the electric stove at our house in

Peoria in order to cling to one piece of my life after returning from New York.

The coffee at work came from a glass pot that sat on a warmer and, undrinkable to begin with, tasted burned after just a few minutes and stayed that way all day. As much as I liked my job and liked Lida and Edna, the coffee made me feel sad and lost.

While proofreading, I thought about how I might solve the problem of the coffee.

The following Monday, I arrived with a thermos filled with coffee I had brewed at home. Behind my desk, for some reason making sure that Edna was not watching (Lida always came in late and stayed late, I assumed a necessary outgrowth of her social schedule), I poured some into a ceramic mug. The first sip was heaven. My problem was solved. I would be happy now, perhaps happy forever. I pictured myself proofreading the yellow pages of telephone books for years and years, sipping excellent coffee, and that seemed a perfectly good life.

That evening, I washed my thermos, and the next morning I made another pot of coffee. At work, the coffee tasted a bit different than it had the day before. It had a faintly metallic flavor.

In the subsequent days, the metallic taste intensified, no matter how well I scrubbed the thermos. I tried a different type of thermos, one with glass lining instead of metal. However, the coffee still tasted odd, and on the second day I dropped the thermos as I rose to leave work for the day. The glass lining shattered.

The following Monday, I arrived early, before either Lida or Edna, carrying a brown paper grocery bag. At my desk, I withdrew a small water heater and set it on the floor behind my desk, next to the wall. In the large lower drawer of my desk, I put a one-cup sized plastic cone, paper coffee filters, a quarter pound of fresh-ground coffee, and a coffee scoop.

I tried to hide my coffee preparation from Edna and Lida, but I quickly realized the water heater's growling and the smell of my grounds would give me away if I made this a daily practice. I did not want them to think I did not respect them or their values. Or worse, I didn't want either of them thinking I did not like them (I loved them) because I did not like the coffee they drank without complaint.

So, at the end of that day, when Edna and Lida were chatting with each other, I loaded my water heater, cone, filters, and coffee back into the grocery bag, and, keeping my body between the bag and my coworkers' view, left for the day.

At home, I tried to talk with Becky about the problem of the coffee, to exchange impressions of the comforting sensation of coffee, to explore other coffee options that did not offend Lida or Edna, but Becky didn't seem interested in that as a topic of conversation.

While proofing the restaurant listings in the Gastonia phone book and trying to determine whether the Chinese character in a display advertisement was right-side up, a thought came to me like a gift: coffee bags! At home that night, I set to work. I used scissors to cut a coffee filter into several flat pieces. I folded the pieces into squares and stapled the edges closed, making small pouches. I poured about one scoop of coffee into each, then stapled closed the top, attaching a piece of string. I felt the buzz of excitement as I cleaned the paper scraps and the dusting of spilled coffee from the kitchen counter, imagining the success and serenity I would experience the next day at work. When I raised my eyes from the garbage can, I saw Becky eyeing me skeptically.

So as not to repeat the problem of the noisy water heater at work, I went into the kitchen and ran hot water from the faucet, which fortunately after a few moments was scalding. At my desk, I dropped in a coffee bag, careful to drape the string outside the cup's rim. I waited one minute, two. The color of the water didn't seem to be changing much beyond a faint beige. I waited one more minute, withdrew the bag, threw it away, and tasted.

The coffee taste barely registered. It tasted the way I imagined sucking on staples would taste.

I settled back in my seat and pulled a set of galley sheets from my basket. I tried to prepare myself for the days ahead.

*

Becky got her hair cut short, got contact lenses, and began to exercise several times each day to a television show she taped called The 20-Minute Workout. Her body changed. Her soft curves flattened, the sense of lightness in her body was replaced by tension and purpose, her eyes and expression seemed to float, but in a dangerous way.

I discovered that Becky didn't know whether Ted Kennedy was a Democrat or a Republican, or whether we lived on the north or south side of the city. These things bothered me, but I kept those feelings private.

Becky enrolled as an undergraduate at North Carolina State University in Raleigh. She chose to major in design. I asked what sort of design that meant, or what sort of design she was interested in, and she said something about architecture but was vague and not inclined to discuss it.

*

Becky and I pulled into the parking lot of the pizza restaurant. I stopped the car and unbuckled my seatbelt, but Becky didn't unbuckle hers.

I didn't always drive when the two of us went out. We did not have a system for determining who drove, nor did the choice get made naturally. It was as though each time we were ready to drive anywhere, the decision was made in some new way, using fresh criteria, with all the awkwardness of a new process, but with no words. It was like two people approaching each other in a narrow hallway and not being able to quite work out how they would pass each other.

Becky said, "I'm not sure about pizza."

I said, "OK."

"It takes a long time."

"It does."

"I just don't feel like sitting for so long."

"That's fine."

"Also, pizza doesn't sound good to me."

I asked, "Where should we go?"

"I don't know."

I looked at her, hoping to read a restaurant preference in her expression. She looked ahead through the windshield.

I started the car and put my seatbelt back on. As I did, I remembered that once she had mentioned that it made more sense to put the seatbelt on before starting the car.

I suggested a family restaurant where we usually ordered Monte Cristo sandwiches.

"OK," she said.

"If the food's not too heavy."

"It's OK."

After pulling into the parking lot, I turned off the car, but did not unbuckle my seatbelt. She did not unbuckle hers, either.

I asked, "What do you think?"

"I'm not sure."

"OK."

"It's awfully bright in there."

"It is."

"And the booths aren't too comfortable."

I said, "That's true. I suppose we could get a table with chairs?"

"Still."

"Yes."

It was summer, rather early, and the idea of going out to dinner in daylight seemed slightly absurd.

I asked, "Any ideas?"

"Mmm."

I thought about the handful of restaurants that we rotated among. For each, I attempted to picture her sitting at a table, ordering, eating—tried to sense how the setting or food would influence her pleasure or acceptance or acquiescence.

I suggested a popular fast-food restaurant, and Becky said yes, but as we approached she said that she thought she might want something nicer. I looked for a clue in the word "nicer."

"I have an idea," I said.

"OK."

The Mediterranean restaurant was on a hill, its parking lot slightly down the hill, and so a bit more exertion than usual was required to walk from the car to the front door.

At the host station, Becky asked to see a menu.

"Mmm," she said.

"The rice dish? You liked it last time."

"I don't know," she said. "I don't really see anything I want."

In the car, I buckled my seatbelt, but Becky did not buckle hers. She began to cry.

She said, "Why didn't you stop me?"

*

I had stolen Becky's life. By coming near me, she had been stained. She had lost friends, college, more friends, a good life. I had taken that away.

*

Becky told me she would have to stay at school late to work on the final project for her principles-of-design class.

When I woke, it took a minute to realize that she was not in bed. Disorientation ballooned around my body. Had she worked all night? I knew that students studied all night for final exams.

However, she had told me that her project was something three-dimensional, something she was constructing. Was it possible to work all night on a sculpture? I had never had to work past eight in the evening, whether studying for a final exam or writing a final paper.

She still wasn't home when I left for work.

That evening, I asked how her project was coming. She said fine. I asked, knowing it was the wrong question, whether she had been working on her project all the time she had been gone. Then I hurried on, trying to obscure that question, saying she must be tired today.

She said she wasn't too tired, that she had taken a nap. She said that most of her classmates were there last night, that they had worked most of the time on their projects and after that just partied for a while.

Party as a verb was a word that people my age seemed to understand instinctively, but that I did not. I assumed that something in the act of partying excluded me, that it involved a level of relaxation, of freedom, of movement, of sensuality, of easy affection that I was not capable of carrying out.

Becky had announced a new and terrifying self-definition, a new and terrifying alignment. She was now—perhaps she had always been—a person who instinctively understood the verb to party, who was able to participate with ease, even eagerness.

I curled and uncurled my toes inside my shoes. Also, I was genuinely curious. I asked what people did when they partied. I was aware that the question made me sound like an old fart, and that the question was a way of stating my alliance with those who did not use party as a verb or did whatever that term denoted.

And a way of hinting at the terror I always felt when seeing an ad in the newspaper for a movie about high school friends or college friends. But I was curious and thought this may be the best, and possibly the last, opportunity I would have to get an answer to the question. The only way I had ever spent time with other people was in conversation. Could partying perhaps just be a way to say talking? I also wanted to know the answer to the question because I wanted to know the degree to which I was losing, or had lost, Becky.

She said, "We just hung around."

That evening, Becky said she had to put some more hours into her project. It would, she said, probably be another all-nighter.

At a few minutes before ten, I left our apartment and drove to the campus. I parked several buildings away from the building where Becky had her class. I took a roundabout route toward the building, in case she should be walking out and see me. It was a long stone building, only three stories tall. I approached from the back, conscious of the darkness around me, looking for evidence of light from windows on either side.

I stepped slowly around the back of the building and saw Becky's car in the parking lot. I imagined her walking with her slightly splayed feet, with her bounce, from the car to the building. I moved toward a broad window showing bright light. The blinds were raised. Even staying to the side, I could see students along long tables, most standing, some talking, some hunched over their work.

Becky was standing at one of the tables. She was holding something that looked like a small box kite, but one that could never fly. Its frame appeared to be dowels on which were placed, at irregular intervals, panels of balsa wood or perhaps fabric painted dusty reds and blues and browns. She held it at eye level, turning it slowly.

It was beautiful. It was light, but somehow still ungainly. It appeared to have no center, no one way to rest on a table or be hung from a string. I imagined Becky letting go and the sculpture still, quiet, before her, just for a moment.

*

I got a little book published, a fictional treatment of my recent years with Steve. I sent the book to Becky's parents, to a few friends, and to relatives. Everyone sent back nice notes, except Grandpa Ray. Two or three weeks later, I got a letter from his wife. Sitting in the living room, I opened it. The typewritten letter began, "We got your book and thank you very much for sending it. However, your grandfather was upset that the book was dedicated to your grandmother rather than to him." I flung away the letter as though it was burning my hands. As I did, I shouted something that was not quite a word. How could I have done something so thoughtless, how could I have not removed the dedication page before sending it to him, how could I have hurt him in this way?

*

I looked at the phone hanging on our kitchen wall. It was new, sleek, white. Becky was away. When I had last used the phone, I had noticed a button I had never seen before. The button was labeled "redial." I thought about what that might mean. I decided it could only mean that pushing the button would call the most recent number dialed. I lifted the handset and pushed the button. A male voice answered. I asked to speak to Becky. He said she wasn't there, paused, and said there was no one there by that name. I hung up. Why, I thought, would a telephone manufacturer put a button like that on a phone?

*

As I sat with Becky in a restaurant, I wondered: What was the difference between a couple sitting quietly and anxiously and a couple sitting quietly and calmly? Could you tell by looking at them? Did they even know themselves?

*

Of course. I was a frozen person. I had isolated Becky from her friends. I had saddled her with a teenage autistic ward. I had dragged her halfway across the country. I was a barely adequate sexual partner. I looked down at the music she liked. I had reduced our lives to going out to dinner and walking in the shopping mall. I was afraid of people who wore bright clothes and danced. My conversation focused mainly on developing arguments for why people who did wear bright colors and dance were somehow flawed, at which I imagined Becky laughing silently and asking herself how anyone could be more deeply flawed than I was.

*

Becky said she got a B+ on her design project.

*

At work, I wrote down things people said on scraps of paper, and I emptied the scraps on my nightstand every night.

*

In Brooklyn as a child, I liked to drink plain seltzer and eat plain matzo. For my birthday one year, Becky bought a contraption to make seltzer at home, but we only used it once.

*

Becky asked to meet me for dinner before I went to teach class. We had been seeing less of each other. She had school, other things to do. Without me, she went to a movie written by, directed by, and starring a flamboyant musician just gaining popularity. I decided that I did not like that musician or that movie, and when I heard mention of either, my stomach knotted and I felt my back begin to sweat.

We met at a counter-service Chinese restaurant near campus. We had only been to this restaurant once, but I liked it a lot.

When we sat, Becky said that she and I needed to see a therapist to work on our communication.

I said OK. I asked her if she was seeing someone else.

She said this issue was the two of us, that we didn't communicate.

I asked whether she was seeing Mark, a name she had mentioned from school.

She said yes.

I asked if she had had sex with him.

She said yes.

I asked whether she wanted a divorce.

She said maybe.

I stood and found the bathroom near the counter. Inside, I threw up. I flushed and stood up. Then I slumped down onto the floor.

Back at our table, I said I had to get to class, which was true.

As I drove to school, I thought about the kiddy-ride horse in front of Woolworth's: I eyed it so longingly for so many years and I understood why my mom always said no because we didn't have a lot of money and if she said yes once we'd expect yes every time and mostly because it was frivolous and would be over in seconds and we probably would just be disappointed but I did admire the smoothness of that horse and its brown and cream-colored streaks and once Mom did say yes and I fully expected to be disappointed but it was gloriously fun, hiccupping up and down, and I never asked again because I knew that was a moment not to be sullied by repetition.

As I drove, I thought about my dad and mom's bed, which was actually two beds pushed together and latched at the foot.

As I drove, I thought about the layers of paving on the streets of Peoria and whether we eventually would have to step up onto the street using small ladders.

As I drove, I thought, well of course; every second I assumed I was going to lose her.

As I drove, I thought that even more than my parents' paintings, I loved the corners, the sides of the unframed, stretched canvases, the paint wrapped around the corner: what it hinted at, what it promised.

As I drove, I thought, I am such a stuffed shirt that I use a phrase like stuffed shirt.

As I drove, I thought about the Sherwood Anderson story "I'm A Fool," the story of a boy who met a wonderful girl but told her so many boastful lies that he realized he could never see her again. I did like that situation, but mostly I liked the title. As I drove, I thought, I'm a fool.

As I drove, I missed Steve.

As I drove home, I remembered that Mom said Dad's marriage proposal consisted only of these words: "We make a good team."

As I drove home, I thought, apparently, I'm not a terribly effective con man.

As I drove home, I finally found the word to describe Becky's father's chuckle: vibrato. Why was that so hard to realize?

As I drove home, I thought: There is a clear difference between a wink of conspiracy and a wink of superiority, and I can tell the difference.

As I drove home, I thought that Mom was right when she would say that I was too young to know what she knew.

As I drove home, I wondered where Becky would be.

*

That night, I tried to have sex with Becky because I was pretty sure when she left, I would never have sex again, but she said we wouldn't solve our problems in the bedroom. She was right, of course. The next night, I stayed in a hotel. At the front desk, I had to sign a waiver because my home address was in the same town and this was the hotel's way of protecting itself against what the clerk called "marital discord."

As I lay in bed, I heard voices. The bedside clock radio said 10:06 PM. The voices rapidly increased in volume. Music started to play. I smelled cigarette smoke.

Becky had seen me many a time at a movie theater fume when people—even all the way across the theater from me— were talking until I would finally, shaking with anger, approach them, and they would look at me with some fear and stop talking, and I would be unable to pay attention to the rest of the movie because I was so embarrassed and so sorry for ruining the movie for the people I had accosted. This time I thought, OK, it's after ten, these people are clearly in the wrong, no waiting necessary.

I was already in a state of constant vibrating anxiety. I was wearing underpants—white briefs—and a button-down shirt and figured, fine, they're not going to see me, I'm just going to knock and tell them to quiet down, so I left my room and in the hallway heard that the sound was directly across from my door, so I had to take only one step forward to knock.

Before I could follow the knock with "hey, keep it down, it's late," the door opened. As if they were waiting for me.

At the door was a young man, perhaps still in high school, and inside the room were other young men wearing gym shorts and college t-shirts, standing around and sitting on a single bed. The boy at the door looked confused, as I supposed he might, faced with another young man, one he didn't know, wearing no pants and a shirt.

I asked, my voice shaking, "Can you turn down the music? It's late, you know."

The boy at the door looked chagrined. He said, "Sure," and the others called from inside the room, "Sorry" and "Sorry, sir."

I turned around, stepped toward my door, turned the handle, pulled, and found that the door was locked. And, being pants-less, I did not have the key. I wondered if being separated from your wife and stuck in a hotel hallway with no key and no pants was a definition of rock bottom.

I glanced back and forth, looking for the elevator. It was to my left, but depressingly far down the hall. I approached it, expecting at any moment to hear the bell of its arrival and to meet a couple departing on my floor who would eye me up and down and snicker or hurry past me. I reached the elevator door without encountering anyone, and when the summoned car arrived and the door slid open, no one was inside.

At the first floor, there was nothing to do but step out of the elevator and hope that no one was nearby. No one was. The elevator opened into a hall with guest rooms. I kept toward the wall as I approached the lobby and saw, within my range of view, no one. The front desk abutted the hallway, and I slid around the counter, which I was thrilled to find was chest high, so, by standing against it, I could shield my lack of pants from the man behind the counter, who was not the suspicious man who had checked me in, but a tall, rounded man with a businesslike haircut and slightly crooked glasses and an air of calm.

I told him that I had locked myself out of my room, and he said, sure, no problem, and what was my room number, and gave me another key, which felt to me like the greatest kindness I had ever received. I slid along the counter and back into the hall, again seeing no one. The elevator door opened, again revealing an empty car. No one in my hallway. Only murmuring from the room across from mine. The key worked. I was inside. I closed the door. I sat on the bed.

*

Reading was impossible. Sleeping in a bedroom was terrifying. I slept on the living room floor. Becky was gone. Every night, I pulled the TV cart close to me and started a videocassette of *Dial M for Murder* I had recorded from television. Lots of talking. Like having a book read to me. The gorgeous young wife played by Grace Kelly was having an affair with an incredibly insipid man played by Robert Cummings. I was pretty sure that the audience was supposed to see the wife as the epitome of charm and, well, grace: She smiled and chatted gayly, and she truly seemed to both love her boyfriend and want to do the right thing by her husband. Still, she kept inviting the boyfriend to parties and drinks with her and her husband, and kissing her husband tenderly in front of the boyfriend, and nobody could convince me she was not cruel. She seemed light light light. Considerations of courtesy and kindness and thoughtfulness, we were to believe, were beneath consideration of a person who is so light.

The woman's husband, urbane, intelligent, articulate, and confident, played by Ray Milland, found out about the affair and blackmailed an old schoolmate into attempting to kill his wife. The plan did not succeed, but the husband brilliantly managed to frame his wife for killing his schoolmate. I could listen to the character forever, he was so smooth and unaffected by his wife's behavior, except of course deciding to kill her.

Later, the husband pulled a bed into the living room, where he slept. Also, he was caught by the insipid boyfriend and a clever and whimsical police inspector. But sometimes I was asleep before this part. If not, I stopped the movie at this point, rewound the tape, and started it over. Even when I slept, I would wake up after an hour or two and start the movie again.

*

I had the four *Nero Wolfe* books that I had chosen to accompany me when my life dissolved. I could not read them. Even if I were able to read them, it would not be sufficient to drown out what needed to be drowned out. I needed not to read the books, but to be inside them so that they were no longer books, but my surroundings and air.

I purchased a portable cassette tape player with a built-in microphone. I bought packages of blank cassette tapes. I inserted a tape, pressed the record and play buttons, and as the leader fed through, I opened the book to the first page. I began to read.

After two paragraphs, I stopped, rewound, and listened.

I was shocked at the sound of my voice. It was flat, dull, like the absence of voice.

I rewound, let the leader run, and started reading again, this time conscious of emphasizing some words, giving my voice dynamics.

After two paragraphs, I stopped, rewound, and played the recording back again. I could barely discern any difference between the first recording and this one.

I tried again, this time using inflections that seemed extreme. I heard some difference, but still the overwhelming impression was of flatness.

Over time, I created a recording that had a reasonable dynamic. I learned how to look ahead so that I was not often tripped up by the words or sentence structures. Having read this book ten or more times, the syntax was familiar, and I usually could find the right points for vocal emphasis. Five cassettes later, when I finished reading the book, I felt as though I had not read it, but instead had both entered it and been consumed by it. I was resting inside it, and it was resting inside me.

While washing the dishes, I listened to the tape. While brushing my teeth, I listened to the tape. I bought a hand-held cassette player with a speaker and held it to my ear while I drove in my noisy car, an awkward proposition given that it was a stick shift, but I got by.

I still listened to the movie *Dial M for Murder* at night, but on nights when I found myself on the third playing of the movie, I would switch to one of my own recordings.

I recorded another book and another. I labeled the tapes not with the names of the books, but with the titles' initials and the number of the tape. I did not want someone to see the tapes and know what they were.

Sometimes, in the car, when the recorded books could not push away throbbing thoughts, I would put a blank tape into the handheld recorder and talk while I drove.

*

Steve and I made pumpkin pies for Thanksgiving. Steve; me—the lowest common denominator, the irreducible minimum.

I had never made pumpkin pies before but thought they came out well. We made two. Steve and I took one and drove to Becky's apartment. She opened her door, and I was conscious of what she was seeing: Steve, me, pie, piteousness.

I told her we could only eat one and wanted to give one to her.

She took it, began to cry, and shut the door.

*

I moved into an apartment on the second floor of a ratty house near downtown Raleigh. The second night, I heard a knock. I opened the door, and a young, thin woman with short, scraggly bleached blonde hair with dark roots stood there. She looked dispirited.

She asked, "Do you have hot water?"

I said, "I think so, but I'm not sure."

She said, "I don't have hot water, and I have to shower before I go to work."

This struck me like a moment straight out of a pulp novel. The only appropriate response was to invite her in to shower in my apartment, and then, with her wrapped in a white towel, another towel wrapped around her hair, to sit in my living room, smoking and drinking bourbon, where we would plan our life on the run together.

I didn't speak. I was tired. I was lost. And she had no idea how worthless I was.

She said, "Oh, well, I can go without showering for one day. See you around."

*

I was talking on the phone with my naked-juggling former roommate. I am not sure what I was saying. I may have been crying. Then I was talking with Becky on the phone. For some reason I thought I had the right to talk with her on the phone, that we would still interact. Pathetic obliviousness. I was repeating a phrase that I didn't even understand as I was repeating it. I was sitting on the floor. The telephone book was on the floor in front of me. So was a pair of pliers. I was hitting the phone book with the pliers. Becky heard the sound and asked me to stop. I repeated the phrase. I was crying. I heard sirens outside. Through my curtains, I saw flashing lights.

I laid the telephone receiver on the floor. I left my apartment, leaning heavily on the stair rail as I slid my feet from stair to stair. On the first floor, I was on my knees, elbows and knees. I crawled toward the door. I reached up and grasped the doorknob. I knew what I would see when I opened the door: an ambulance, maybe an ambulance and a police car, people walking from their vehicles toward the door, there to take me. OK, I said aloud. OK. I opened the door. No one was there.

*

It was a lovely but hot summer in Raleigh—nothing new there. The city was still, comfortably oblivious to my existence.

The man had answered my ad about the car and, over the phone, said the price sounded fair. He said he wanted a car for his daughter. He said he wanted to be sure that she had a safe car, and that a Toyota Corolla should be safe for her.

The man's house was every house of every one of my elementary school acquaintances, only perhaps a bit larger, the lawn a bit tidier.

The man's house had two stories, white aluminum siding, brown faux shutters, thin white pillars. Inside, everything was flat and clean and unmemorable.

The man was perhaps in his late forties, which seemed middle-aged to me. Trim, good handshake and smile-lined face.

I had to explain to him that the car now had a crack in the front bumper. My wife had driven it into a post in a parking lot in the two days since I had first spoken to the man. I did not tell him that. He and I stepped outside, and he looked at the bumper and said he thought it wouldn't be expensive to fix and agreed to the lower price I suggested. He drove the car, returned, and we sat in his living room.

He asked what I did, and I told him I was a proofreader for a printing company.

He asked why I was selling the car. I told him that I was moving away from Raleigh, that I was moving to Chicago, that I would not need a car there.

"Starting over?" he asked.

"I guess so," I said.

He said that was a good thing to do when you were still young.

I asked what he did. He said he was in charge of computers at a regional insurance company.

I said that the job seemed like a lot of responsibility.

"Computers," he said, "are just a way to make more mistakes faster."

He gave me a check, and we shook hands.

He smiled. He glanced around his living room, glanced at his kids in the kitchen. "In a way," he said, "I envy you."

*

In the group home's living room, I sat with one of the part-time managers. I had never met her and forgot her name as soon as she said it. She told me she was a college student. I sat on one end of the couch. She sat in a chair at the far corner of the room, her legs crossed.

Via telephone, I had already told the group home supervisor, and I had already told the head of the autism agency. And now, I was telling the manager on duty. I realized even as I started to speak that there was no reason to tell this person, who would probably be gone when the semester ended.

I told her things she couldn't possibly care about. I told her that I could not find the kind of job I wanted in North Carolina. I told her I would have better luck in a big city. I told her that I didn't have any friends in North Carolina but I had a friend in Chicago. I told her that I dreaded telling Steve, but that we would see each other a lot. "That poor kid," I said. "His dad dead, his mom dead." My voice broke. "Moving from his home. Now this." Tears rolled out. "How many more horrible things is he going to have to hear?"

The part-time manager twisted in her chair and looked at the carpet.

In Steve's room, we sat on his bed, side by side, our legs over the side, our feet on the floor.

I asked Steve whether he liked Chicago.

"Yes," he said, "I like Chicago."

I asked Steve whether he liked Chapel Hill.

"Yes," he said, "I like Chapel Hill."

I told Steve I liked Chicago and Chapel Hill, too. I told him that I was going to move to Chicago.

"You're going to move to Chicago?"

I told him that he would be able to visit me in Chicago.

"I'll visit you in Chicago?"

And I told him I would visit him in Chapel Hill.

"You'll visit me in Chapel Hill?"

I got down to details, the contract. I would call him every week on Sunday. He would take a plane and visit me every Thanksgiving and every Christmas. I told him that every summer, around his birthday, he could pick a place for us to drive, even if it was a long drive.

"When will we go to Peoria?"

I told him when he was in Chicago, we could drive to Peoria any time he wanted.

I asked, "How does that sound?"

He said, "A little good."

2016-2018

On a flight to North Carolina, before the plane took off, the young woman in the window seat turned to me and asked, "Where are you from?"

I said, "Chicago."

"Where you live with...?"

I said, "No one."

"Are you divorced?"

I said, "Yes," then added, "twice."

She said, "Why?"

*

After my second wife asked me for a divorce, and after we had sold the house, I was excited about living in a small apartment, sometimes with my younger son and sometimes alone. Our family house had been too large, too full of awkwardly configured and usually unoccupied spaces. Small sounded like a good thing. Small sounded like a way to go unnoticed. Not so much to disappear as to reconnoiter, regroup.

I may, however, have taken this idea of small too far.

My younger son was with me every other week, and during one stay he asked if I would buy him a larger bowl. "For the way I eat, I need a little more space," was the way he phrased it, which was nice, I thought, putting the responsibility on himself.

Last week, however, when he asked me to buy him a larger coffee cup, his tone was a little sharper, carried a hint of "what's with you and these tiny cups?"

Small applied not only to the size of my cups, but the quantity of my dishware. I owned three plates, three bowls, and three cups. One for me, one for my son, and one extra. When I had found them at a local resale shop, I covered my face to hide what I'm sure was a goofy smile. Not only could I buy them individually rather than in a set, not only did they have the same floral border as the plates of my Lawrence Welk-loving great aunts in Brooklyn, but also and most important, they were small.

(In the same thrift shop I also found a small table, which turned out to be both comically too tiny for my dining room and weirdly heavy, as if it were made of iron, much to the dismay of my good-natured older son, who bore most of the weight as we carried it up four flights of stairs.)

With a small plate or bowl or cup, I thought, eating or drinking would never become rote. I wouldn't tire of a meal. Within a small container, each experience would be still and perfect—like a soap bubble poised in the air. Standing in the resale shop, small plates, bowls, and cups in my hands, I saw before me an infinite number of still and perfect moments.

Nevertheless, I took my son's point. Small could pose problems.

I had to be extra careful not to spill when carrying a tiny, full cup from the kitchen to the dining room.

One weekend, a bartender, his professional friendliness

fraying, told me, "Someday I am going to get you to order a full beer."

Also, I remembered in graduate school a professor telling me it was a miracle every time I wrote one of my small stories because of all I disallowed.

But I was pretty sure this current small was not a permanent small. As I said: reconnoitering, regrouping.

*

In the past few years, Steve's thing has been to cough. Not a physiological cough, but an autism cough.

It started as a kind of dry gagging cough that he would do before he spoke. I could imagine his pleasure in the tickling sensation deep down in his throat. The cough was just another tic, also another way to buy time for him to formulate words and sentences. In previous years, before speaking, he would make a quiet "nuh nuh nuh nuh"—always four. In years before that, he would say his first word, then whisper that word four times, as if testing it for further use.

I hated the gagging sound. I hated it on the phone each week, when I would wince at the blast in my ear and ask him to turn his mouth away from the receiver when he coughed, an instruction I knew was futile. I hated the gagging sound when he visited and the sound exploded out of him after a period of silence when I approached him with a question, no matter how gently enunciated. And I hated it especially when we were trapped in the car together, taking one of Steve's interminable drives to see some obscure point on an interstate highway or some tollway service plaza, and the gagging seemed to echo inside the car.

When Steve visited me, I was thrilled when each night I could finally retreat to my room. When we were traveling on one of his summer trips—always just the two of us, never my wife or children—I was thrilled when we could return to the hotel room, where for a while I could leave him alone with his maps and brochures, and I could take a walk. And when I visited Steve in North Carolina, I was thrilled each night when I dropped him off at the group home. Before returning to my hotel room, I would find a tiny bar where I sat quietly, read, and drank, very slowly, a tiny glass of bourbon.

*

During the week, I would plan my routes. On weekends when my younger son was not with me, I drove. I drove south. At first, I drove quickly to escape the rubber-band pull of Chicago and its suburbs. Then I drove slowly on state and county highways, each evening stopping at a tiny bar, where I always knew I was in the right place when I felt the crunch of a gravel parking lot beneath my tires and, when I got out of the car, the tiny rocks beneath my feet.

*

1973. Family vacation, Lake of the Ozarks.

When our family emerged in the dark from the tree-crowded gravel road, we saw a low, long house lighted by one arc light. The house was covered in dirty white siding and was indistinguishable from any Peoria house, except for the black blank beyond it, which I assumed was the lake, and the shoulder-high wooden sign, to one side of the road, lighted from beneath, stating the name of the resort.

Dad got out from the driver's seat, and I heard the crunch of his shoes on the gravel parking lot. I followed him, my feet making a higher-pitched version of Dad's crunching steps. Dad opened the wooden screen door, its green paint flaking off, and we entered.

Inside was a bar. I had seen bars in movies but had never been in one. Browns and greens, signs lighted and not, a dozen or two bottles and labels, wood bar top and steel-legged and vinyl-topped stools coalesced in a gentleness, a calm. Two couples sat at the bar.

The white-shirted bartender drifted toward my dad, and they began to go through the transaction of our checking in for a week's vacation. To the right of the bar, I saw a flat surface leading toward a lighted sign like a pinball machine, only this appeared to be a bowling machine. I touched the flat surface, first just a tap with my fingertips, and then drawing my fingertips across the surface. The bartender leaned over the bar, reached out, and dropped several quarters into a slot. The machine emitted some low-volume chimes, the lights began to flash slowly, and a wooden puck emerged from somewhere. I held the puck and looked at the machine.

"Push it," a voice said. I turned and saw that one of the couples was watching me. "Toward the pins," the man said.

I turned back to the machine. Plastic replica bowling pins

had dropped down from the end of the machine. I placed the puck on the flat surface and pushed it toward the pins.

I was startled at how smoothly the puck traveled along the surface, as naturally as breathing, as though there were no friction. The puck veered to the side, but crossed under one pin, which flipped back.

The puck reemerged, and I pushed it again, feeling a deep thrill at how my gentle propulsion resulted in such quick and sleek travel for the puck. This time the puck passed under the center of the pins, and all but one flipped up. I heard a few claps and a call of support from the bar.

During the vacation, we swam and fished and went out in a rented rowboat with an outboard motor. But mostly, I wanted to be in the white building. I realized that I had seen bars like this—bars that looked like houses—everywhere in Peoria, but that they were places where others went, not us, not me.

*

Lacon, Illinois. Evening.

Across 5th Street, which is the main street in this town, young kids gathered in a parking lot. Their voices scattered like polite fireworks into the quiet. Two kids moved away from the group, orbiting briefly, before returning.

I passed The Coffee Hub, brightly lit but about to close. I had been there earlier in the day. The space that The Coffee Hub occupied could barely contain its energy. The walls were covered with rolls of butcher block paper, on which were written not words but celebrations: 31 flavor shots for your coffee! Oatmeal with dried cherry berry blend! 16 flavors of Uncle Bob's ice cream! Real old-fashioned bottled sodas! Tuna or chicken salad on croissant or Kaiser roll! Orange, apple, and pineapple juice! 11 varieties of homemade fudge! Peach pie! Local coffee! Employee of the week! Local music! Charity of the month! One portion of a wall was crowded with paintings by a local artist, another with historic photos. Just now, an employee was removing a standing sign from the sidewalk near the front door, which said, "Is your name Lane? Come get your FREE ice cream!"

I passed the Marshall County Historical Society. Thanks to the streetlight, I could read the covers of the three old books displayed in the storefront, all written by a deceased local resident named Delight Bobilya Wier. One was titled *Diary of a Farmer's Wife*, another *I Married a Farmer*, and the last *Circle of Love: A Tribute to Farm Women*.

I passed three firemen, each leaning in a slightly different direction on a bench outside the fire station.

I passed the small grocery store with its hand-painted signs announcing the special prices that day for cantaloupes and sirloin steak. I loved the huge painted letters and numbers. My dad, to supplement his teacher's salary, used to paint signs like these for grocery stores windows in Peoria. Or so I had been told. This was before I had been born. If I had seen the grocery-store signs that my dad painted, I knew that I would have recognized my dad's warmth in those huge letters and words.

At all times, the shadowy bridge ahead reminded me of the Illinois River below.

I turned onto Washington Street, toward the too-small blue sign that hung over Linda Lou's 119, where the two women who tended bar were never quite sure how much to charge me for my drink. "How much did we charge last time?" one usually said. "We just kind of make it up," the other usually replied.

On the wall behind the bar, next to the antique cash register (which they still used, when they bothered to ring up a sale) was one of my favorite homemade signs: "No personal checks will be taken here. You have done this—not I."

I sat next to an unoccupied stool in front of which was a half-full pitcher of beer. It was early, so I just ordered a beer from the bartender, whom I was surprised to note was a young woman I had never seen there before. I received my beer in a clear plastic cup. A young man approached and sat in front of the half-empty pitcher. He turned his whole body to face me and shook his head. "I just never expected to see anyone like you in here."

He rested his head on the bar.

When he lifted his head, he continued. "I'm from Kuwait. I'm a truck driver. I'm only twenty-three. Have you ever been to Kuwait?"

I told him that I hadn't.

"If you move there, you'll make a lot more money than you make here." He gestured toward the pitcher of beer. "This is my second, and I'm not going to be able to finish it, if you want some."

He turned to the bartender. "What's that design on your leggings?"

"It's from a band."

"What band?"

"The Misfits."

"I don't know them. Do you like rap music?"

"No," she said, "I like Bob Dylan and the Velvet Underground."

"I've never heard of them."

"They're old. I guess I'm an old soul."

I finished my cup of beer and, because it was still early, left. In the alley next to Linda Lou's, a group of older teenagers was having footraces. Shouts echoed, and a boy and girl tore down the alley. After they stopped and a winner was declared, a couple of the teenagers looked up toward the two-story roof of Linda Lou's. Three or four kids were standing at the edge. Someone from the ground yelled, "Why are you up there?" Someone from the roof yelled, "Why anything?"

A shape launched from the roof. The streetlight captured a glow against the dark sky. It was a clear plastic cup. It floated up and then began its arc. At that moment, glittering drops began to spread and fall.

*

Steve and I were sitting next to one another on the group home couch. I had just arrived from the airport. He was holding his shoes, ready to put them on so we could go out for a drive. I chatted with one of the managers, and the other residents wandered in and out of the room, saying hello to me and asking the manager for this and that. The group home was the most cheerful place I knew. A place without inhibitions. A home in the fullest sense.

As usual, Steve did not participate in the conversation, but bounced subtly, happily, as the activity went on around him. I saw that, as always, Steve's left big toe was fully exposed, poking out from a hole in his sock.

For many years, Steve always had a hole in his sock in the spot that should have covered his left big toe. Frequently, the hole spread so that all his toes on that foot were exposed. Every time I saw Steve I bought him new socks. When he was visiting, I asked Steve to give me the socks with holes so I could throw them away. When I was at the group home, he and I went through his drawers and, asking permission from Steve—who would touch each pair twice with his fingertips, and sometimes took the pair and touched it once to his cheek—I took away his holey socks. Usually I threw them away at my hotel so he couldn't retrieve them from the garbage. Sometimes I mailed Steve new socks—and jeans and underwear and shirts—but I was never sure he wore them. It was very difficult to introduce new pieces into Steve's clothing rotation.

In the earlier days of Steve's sock-hole habit, I sometimes saw a bit of blood on his sock near the exposed toe, but, examining his feet, I could never find the source. I always assumed the holes were caused by his toenails needing to be clipped. Vaguely, I would wonder why the holes only appeared in the left sock, but I never thought about that for more than a few minutes, having long ago stopped seeking logical explanations for the phenomena that surrounded Steve.

I said, "Hey, Steve. How about you put those shoes on so we can…" Here I paused with over-obvious drama that Steve seemed to like, "…go for a drive!"

"Yes!" Steve said. "Go for a drive!"

As Steve slipped on his tennis shoes—a pair I had sent him a few months ago—another manager entered the room, and we started another line of conversation. Steve, shoes on, sitting on my left, sat back and crossed his legs, left ankle on right knee, and jiggled his left foot.

I glanced over and saw a hole the size of a half-dollar in the sole of his shoe, just at the big toe. And I saw his bare big toe through the hole.

I always tried not to embarrass Steve, but an "Ah!" escaped me. Two thoughts fought for right of way in my mind. "How did you get that hole?" came out of my mouth first.

"I don't know," Steve said, the words running together, as he slapped his foot flat on the floor so I couldn't see the hole.

I let the second thought out: "So that's why you get holes in your socks!"

It was like the denouement of a whodunnit. But even as that feeling was registering, I was already questioning my conclusion. Why had I never seen holes in the soles of his shoes before? Well, the soles always faced the floor, but still, in all the years Steve's big toe had been exposed from a holey sock, would I never have seen the sole of Steve's left shoe?

As this and other questions pecked at my thoughts, one of the managers made his own exclamation: "Ah!"

I turned toward him.

"I know how that happened!" he said. "Yesterday. I saw Steve on his bike. Down at the end of the driveway. And he was stopping the bike with his foot!"

Steve was squirming, as he always did when anyone mentioned his behaviors, and I patted his knee and then his shoulder. I considered it my greatest accomplishment, a plenty good reason to have lived a life, that Steve no longer flinched from my touch.

I said to the manager, "And his brakes are always getting broken." I turned to Steve. "Are your brakes broken again? Were you stopping your bike with your foot?" Although Steve regularly told me his brakes weren't working, and I regularly arranged to pay for the repairs, I imagined that perhaps his brakes malfunctioned even more often than he let on, and not wanting to sacrifice his bike rides, Steve was not telling anyone and using his foot instead. I pictured him coasting into an oncoming car, unable to make a hard stop with his foot on the pavement.

"Oh well," I said to Steve, "I know one thing we'll be doing during this visit. Buying you new shoes and socks!" I tried to make it sound like a party.

"Buying me new shoes and socks," Steve said.

As we drove that afternoon, the satisfaction of having solved a mystery started to decay. I had just paid to repair Steve's bike, so why was he stopping with his foot yesterday? And if he was stopping his bike with his foot, and if he had worn a hole in his shoe sole, why was his toe not bloody? And had this really been happening for so many years?

That night, I drove to the outskirts of town for a drink. In the bar, a man shouted, "Now this guy," pointing at me, "if I were to steal this guy's wallet, that would just be a sign of my low self-esteem. See, if I stole this guy's wallet, I would be saying that this guy has his shit together enough to have three hundred dollars, but I only have my shit together enough to have three dollars."

People around the bar laughed, and so did I. The man called to me, "Do you have a condo in Durham?"

I told him no.

Later, as he was presumably heading for the bathroom, the man paused at my stool, put his hand on my shoulder, and whispered into my ear, "I still think you have a condo in Durham." That night, sitting up in bed in my hotel room, I again saw Steve's foot—the hole in his shoe sole, the bare toe visible through the hole.

I thought, I know how Steve will die.

I didn't know exactly, but that was the point.

I knew some private behavior, some unknown activity, would twist inside him, like a tiny dagger, and then one day, Steve would just expire. His expiration would be a mystery to anyone not inside his mind or his body. But that wouldn't matter. He would be dead.

*

I had no close friends when I was married. Trying to repair that post-divorce, I renewed acquaintance with a man who as an adult had taken several college writing classes with me many years before.

He was a serious reader, a serious writer, a serious photographer, a world traveler. He now lived in Las Vegas. He was also dying of breast cancer. We exchanged messages multiple times each day. He told me that the only place he hadn't visited that he really wanted to visit was India, but that was OK. He told me that he took only short walks and not every day, that he took a few photos, but only with his phone. He told me that he couldn't pay attention well enough to read anymore; instead, he lay on the couch watching DVDs of the 1970s TV show *Hart to Hart.*

I told my friend that I had business in Las Vegas, but I didn't. I flew from Chicago into the Las Vegas airport and drove a rental car out to a new strip mall that seemed all alone near some hazy-looking mountains, and I walked into a snappy-looking coffee shop, where I knew he went most days to get his espresso.

I arrived first and soon saw a thin body silhouetted in the doorframe and knew from the ironic tilt of the head that this was my friend.

As we drank, he told me that when he got his cancer diagnosis, he thought everything would stop in deference to his situation, but that his boss still thought he had a bad attitude, and he still had problems with his partner, and he still had to pay his bills. He also told me that one day in this coffee shop, sitting at the table he and I sat at now, he started crying and couldn't stop, and the guy behind the counter came over and comforted him.

I pictured my friend lying on his side on a couch, upholstered in scratchy fabric in a sunny living room with slippery plastic, *Hart to Hart* DVD cases scattered on the carpet. I imagined him imagining himself riding shotgun with Jonathan and Jennifer Hart as they zipped through the streets of LA in their red Dino 246 GTS, scooping up bad guys between shopping trips at Gucci and cocktails at Chasen's. And all things considered, that seemed OK to me.

After my dad died, my aggressively non-TV-watching mom

moved a portable black-and-white set into her bedroom, where she lay under the covers, drank gin, and watched The Rockford Files, admitting to me that she found James Garner handsome. I imagined her imagining herself unbuttoning James Garner's white shirt. And that seemed OK to me.

After Grandpa Ray died, I went to visit his widow, the one whom I had been instructed not to call Grandma Dorothy, at their house in Port Townsend. My memories of the house were of a place where I was instructed to turn down the volume of the Rolling Stones' *Exile on Main Street* and where one room was actually called The Library. In my grandfather's bedroom closet, on a high shelf, I found stacks of paperback *Nero Wolfe* mystery novels. I imagined my grandfather imagining himself as an in-demand, all-knowing detective dealing crushing rejoinders in high Wolfe-ian style to the intellectual inferiors all around him, rather than as a pompous irrelevancy the world now happily ignored. And that seemed OK to me.

As I sat drinking coffee with my dying friend, I made a pledge to watch *Hart to Hart*—episode after episode—as soon as I returned home.

*

I kept a list of my favorite conversations overheard in barrooms:

"I've been a nanny for a long time. It pays my bills. It's ridiculously lucrative and ridiculously easy. But I want to be a high school Frisbee teacher. Did you know a lot of fat people play Frisbee? I mean, a wide range of body types. If I could be a high school drama and Frisbee teacher, I would do that in a heartbeat."

"I haven't seen these in months," said by a girl withdrawing a pair of thong underwear from her jacket pocket.

"If only I had a girlfriend for one week each year, and that week was Christmas, that would be OK."

"I just won twenty-six thousand dollars. Have a cheeseburger."

*

At the airport, as I guided Steve through security to return to North Carolina, when he had to take off and then put back on his belt, he pulled his shirt up high, exposing his belly from just above his low-hanging pants up to his breastbone. How wonderful, I thought, to live a life without modesty. And I thought, look at that flat belly. Look at those muscles. How could this guy be in his mid-fifties? And I thought, how long will he be able to keep riding his bike? And what will he do when he can't ride his bike?

I noticed that Steve was getting thinner. He looked as though he were shrinking to his minimum self, a self that was one set of hard bicycle-riding muscles. He always had a tan, but it no longer made him look healthy.

He ate well at the group home. I mean, boy did he eat. No one ate as much as Steve. And he loved to talk about what he ate. On our calls (every Sunday night at 7 PM, and I caught hell if I ever was late: "You didn't call me. Where were you? You didn't call me. I was so worried."), I always started with,

"How was your weekend?" and Steve would list every activity, including every item in every meal or snack the whole weekend.

Also, the group home managers made sure he didn't ride his bike on the hottest days, and lately they made sure he didn't go out for more than a half hour at a time, and no more than twice each day.

The group home supervisor called me one day and started with, "First, everything is all right."

Being familiar with these kinds of telephone calls, I felt both numb and relaxed, knowing I would be equal to whatever information was coming.

The night before, Steve had fainted in the bathroom. He had fallen, hitting the back of his head on the sink. He had been bleeding. An ambulance took him to the hospital. He got staples in his head. The doctors saw no underlying problem. He was home now.

A week later, the same thing happened. He fainted, hit his head, bled, went to the hospital, returned home—no apparent cause.

Two days later, it happened again.

Then it didn't happen anymore.

*

After I moved to Chicago, in the years before I met my second wife, the holidays were defined by Steve and me. Just Steve and me. As the world seemed to revel around us, or huddle in warm homes packed with loved ones, Steve and I walked through the snowy, half-empty Chicago Loop so he could see the buses and the elevator in the Thompson Center and the top floor of the new library. We visited the top of the Hancock Center (where there was a place for me to sit) and the Sears Tower (where there wasn't) so Steve could spend as long as I could tolerate and then a little longer looking at the city streets from above. We drove and drove and drove through dirty mist that my windshield wipers could never quite remove, all in order to see distant spots on interstate highways.

Our holiday dinners were serviceable at best. Once we ate Christmas dinner—or was it Thanksgiving dinner?—at a service plaza suspended over an interstate highway, chewing our McDonald's burgers (his with, as he forcefully told the girl at the counter, "no cheese and no mayonnaise"—the proper fulfillment of which he checked with trembling fingers as soon as the bag was handed to us) while overlooking the cars that rushed beneath us.

In the earlier years, Paul would join us, but later he got married, and a few years later his wife forbade Paul from seeing either Steve or me. That went on for about twenty years.

Even after I remarried, even after the kids were born, the holidays still were Steve and me. Oh, Steve and I joined the family for Thanksgiving dinner and to open Christmas presents and to light Hanukkah candles (if he was there for Hanukkah) and to watch the ball drop in Times Square on New Year's Eve (while the rest of the family slumped in our chairs and rubbed our eyes, Steve would perform the countdown with gusto, and then jump, wave his hands, and proclaim "Happy New Year," and I would do what I could to accompany him). But most of the hours put in over the holidays were Steve and me on our outings.

Now that I was single again, more than ever, I felt the finality of Steve and me as the lowest common denominator, as the irreducible minimum.

*

At work, I had just returned to my office from the restroom. I sat, leaned back, and tried to reenter the task I had been encompassed by before my restroom trip. I put my feet up on my wastebasket and saw that a strip of toilet paper about ten inches long was stuck to my right shoe. Clearly, it had trailed me all the way from the restroom, which was quite a stroll from my office.

I started to snicker and then I started to laugh. I shut my door, although it had a large pane of glass, so I was still basically in public. Also, the walls were thin, but my office neighbor had told me at least a year before that she was used to the strange sounds that came from my office. I couldn't stop laughing. I thought about pretending to be on the phone, but that seemed a pretty lame pretext for laughing, so I just turned around and looked at the parking lot out my window.

Aunt Norma and Uncle Jerry's ranch house in Valley Stream, Long Island, had low ceilings, even viewed by an undersized seven-year-old, and apparently there was something equally foreign to me about the dimensions of their toilet. Because of that, I soaked my pants during an attempt to use their bathroom. What Do I Do and How Did This Happen ricocheted around in my head as I unrolled a handful of toilet paper to dab at my underpants and pants.

I soon realized that my dabbing did little good and that the visible wetness seemed limited to my underwear.

I stuffed more toilet paper between underpants and pants, then sniffed the air around me to determine how obvious my mistake would be to others. I smelled nothing, but there surely was a smell, and therefore I was unable to smell the odor of my own urine.

Back in the family room, toilet paper padding my crotch and butt area, I kept to one side of the gathering, wishing the room were bigger so that more neutral air surrounded me, but glad that we weren't in the confined space of the car.

As the gathering shifted position in the house, slowly, slowly, like the sleeper in the Andy Warhol movie, I rotated my own position for maximum distance. I looked for any signs of odor-related reaction in the faces of those around me—Aunt Norma and Uncle Jerry, whom I feared possibly offending with my filth; Mom, whom I did not want to supply with fresh ammunition for her view of me; Dad, wanting to bank his good will for some more significant occasion; and Paul, who would do his big-brother job of teasing me if he knew. Steve was, alas, behaving well for a change. I could usually rely on him to take attention away from me.

As the evening wound down, I allowed myself to believe that I had escaped the infamy, until Aunt Norma tossed a glance in my direction as I stood near the front door. She tilted her head down a quarter of an inch, transformed the glance into a stare, and said with the throaty voice I found so deliciously exotic, "You're leaking toilet paper."

I looked down to where her gaze seemed directed, and sure

enough, toilet paper hung from the right leg of my pants. I imagined myself pulling at the hanging piece and it emerging like an endless handkerchief from a magician's breast pocket.

Raising my eyes, I saw this: Aunt Norma, looking back at me with an expression that said I'm confused as shit, but I'm not going to enter the absurd, private predicament of this seven-year-old boy.

Now chuckling, a lifetime later, I pulled the toilet paper from my shoe, dropped it into the wastebasket, and turned back to my work.

*

Steve's dry gagging cough became a phlegmy cough, surely from fluid attempting to relieve the constant scratching at the back of his throat. On top of that came a new kind of cough. This one sounded like he was attempting to blow air through a swollen trachea.

Our phone conversations had followed a tight pattern for many years. I would say, "How was your weekend?" He would say, "Great!" I would say, "What did you do this weekend?" And, punctuated by an occasional single cough blast, he would list each event and meal.

Now, I would say, "How was your weekend?" and he would cough—the gagging kind.

He would say, "Well," clear his throat, and cough again—the phlegmy kind. Again, he would say, "Well…" and again cough. "Well…" Now a constricted-airway cough. "Well, good but…" another cough, "good but not good."

The chronology of his weekend would follow, slowly, often with only a single word between coughs. At the appropriate point, the not-good part would arrive, accompanied by a collision of constricted-airway coughs: It rained one day so he couldn't ride his bike. Or the internet went down for a few hours. Or the manager he expected on a certain day was replaced by another manager. Or the van needed repair so they couldn't go on an outing. Or his DVD player wasn't working.

At the end of the weekend report, he would repeat the not-good portion and say his new favorite phrase: "And that's the problem."

And sometimes, perhaps every month or two, he would say he wasn't comfortable living in the group home, where it always rained or the internet always went down or the managers who were supposed to be there never were or the van always broke down or his DVD player never worked. He would say he loved me and he wanted to live with me in Chicago, where it didn't rain all the time or he wouldn't have to worry about the managers or my car never broke down or my DVD player always worked.

Somehow, we would find a slender reed to grasp onto. I would remind him that next month was the North Carolina State Fair. Or I told him I would send him a new DVD player. Or I asked him to tell me about a new highway video on YouTube. Or we agreed that after we got off the phone, we would both have an ice cream bar for a snack before bed. Or I would ask Steve to tell me where he wanted to visit when we got together in August.

Then, with the most beautiful lilt, with the most relaxing

cadence, with the two notes at the end of the most comforting bedtime song, Steve would say just this: "All right."

AUGUST 2018

Driving along the Illinois River toward Peoria. Three parallel lines: road, train tracks, river. A gray day. Early fall.

The road and train tracks are raised. Glancing away from my driving, I look down at the smattering of houses on the stretch of land that is separated from the river by the road and train tracks.

There are no trees. No fences. Viewed from above, the houses are exposed. They are naked.

From many, the content appears to have spilled out—chairs, couches, toys that can be ridden or sat in, pets, tables, cars, trucks, boats. No, "spilled out" is not right. Rather, it is as though, in this neighborhood by the river, a house is not considered the sole container of one's life. A house is like another chest of drawers. Possessions can be inside or out. Life can move fluidly between both.

However, I see no people.

Inside the neighborhood, the drive along the long street is like a tracking shot in an art-house movie.

I see two cushioned rocking chairs on a lawn, side by side. Leaves and inscrutable debris have collected beneath the chairs. The debris and the seats of the chairs are almost touching. I imagine the years that have passed, the arc of rocking diminishing annually. Now, the chairs would be able to rock a few inches at best. Within several years, the chairs will disappear entirely.

A white house seems longer than the others, but also low, so low it is hard to imagine the inhabitants being able to stand up straight. This is our old neighborhood, so I know that a girl who lived there became part of the ensemble of a popular television show and continues to pop up in various roles, although her career has quieted as she has come to fully occupy middle age. My brother Paul used to babysit her.

The street signs are a different color than they were last year.

The yellow house, the house from which the family escaped so many years ago, has brown trim. The house appears soft. The brown trim appears soft. Were I to touch either, it would be the consistency of cake frosting.

Across the street, the trees in front of our house are gone. They have been gone for many years. There is no sign of their ever having existed.

The redwood is gone. Instead, there is deliriously ugly light blue siding, a light blue that even the owners, upon seeing it covering their house, would have to stare at a moment, shake their heads, perhaps grin and shrug.

The picture window has a shadowy curtain inside.

On the lawn next to the house is a large white boat on a trailer. Next to the boat, taller than the house, is a bus the size and type that a moderately successful rock band would use on tour. It is a soupy, swirling brown. Its driver's side front bumper is coated with layers of duct tape.

Directly in front of the house is a tiny Triumph sports car, in its potency somehow larger than the bus, boat, and house.

I picture a rock band returning from tour in the dead of

night, spilling out of the bus, the band members stumbling giddily toward the house, except for one or two, who hop into the Triumph and zoom down the road, along the river, toward the all-night convenience mart for beer.

The vehicles overwhelm the house. Driving past, I can only think about a cartoon I once saw of a muscle-bound man walking a tiny dog.

I ask Steve where he wants to go now. He will never tell me a destination, only the next turn. And the next. Sometimes I ask how far we are going, and he says, "I don't know" or "We'll see."

Steve has a list of places he sees every year when we visit Peoria. We don't see every place each year, but we see most of them, and those we don't one year he remembers and puts at the top of his list for next year. The places are sometimes sites like a day camp he attended but more often a stretch of highway that was built twenty or more years ago and that is now being repaved and the lines repainted, perhaps for the second or third time.

He directs me toward a part of East Peoria that he and I have never visited together. I see a smattering of gas stations and strip malls, but they soon give way to a string of homes interrupted occasionally by a house converted into a sundry shop or a tailor or a psychic reading parlor or a tavern. It is early afternoon but gray. Peoria is always gray.

Earlier in the day, we passed the apartment where Steve and Becky and I lived. It is a permanent item on Steve's list. Every time we pass, my legs feel soft and weak. They felt soft and weak today as well. But instead of driving past earlier, as I usually do—and which is enough for Steve, who just wants to check sites off his list—I pulled to the curb and invited Steve to get out. I showed Steve how to take a picture with my iPhone, and I stood in front of the building, in front of Becky's and my bedroom window. I did an open-mouthed smile, and Steve took a picture.

Nearby was Bradley University, and I parked near the quad, and Steve and I walked to the dorm where I had stolen a twenty-dollar bill. I set up my phone, handed it to Steve, stood in front of the dorm and smiled a big one. He took a picture.

Steps away was the sculpture by our family friend, the sculpture that my mother said was too small. She was right. It was too small. Whatever. I liked the sculpture; I liked that it was too small. Everything in Peoria is awkwardly scaled. I handed Steve the phone and posed.

We usually stop at the McDonald's on Main Street near the university for lunch. Today, I tell him I have a different restaurant in mind for lunch. We stop at a building that looks like a shed, in a neighborhood that used to be between other neighborhoods. The building has been there since we were kids, unchanged. It always had cars beside and in front of it. I assumed it was a bar or a restaurant, other kids had mentioned that their parents went there, but to me it was always a mystery, a place where people not of my mother's class went, its nondescriptness making its promise all the more tantalizing and hard to imagine.

Inside is a long wooden bar with a smattering of men and women on dark red stools. The clouds have scattered, and light probes through chinks in the curtains. Families and couples sit on standard red vinyl banquet chairs at square tables with checked tops. Two boys playing one arcade game are crammed into a corner. I suggest to Steve that we eat at the bar. Oh, the fried chicken is delicious. OK, it's a little bland, but its blandness is delicious. The owner stops by to chat. It turns out he is from the part of Chicago where I live. We talk for fifteen or twenty minutes. I ask Steve to take a picture of the two of us, and then I take a picture of him with Steve.

Now Steve is watching the surroundings intently as usual, head snapping here and there for no apparent reason. Traffic is moving quickly. Only houses surround us. The two-lane road winds. The dull gray pavement is patched in long, twisting, intersecting strips of tar, so many strips that I assume the only reason the road hasn't been repaved is that the city has given up on it.

I ask Steve where we are going to turn, and he says, "We'll see." I ask if we are close. I am beginning to get impatient. We seem to be going into the middle of nowhere. I want to turn around and go to the hotel. Steve will look at videos of highways on my laptop, and I will take a walk downtown. He says, "We'll see."

He tells me to turn. I slow as he hesitates, as he always does when trying to figure out left from right. "Left," he says.

As I turn, I glimpse, on a wooden post, a tiny rectangular sign that says WEEK-TV. We turn onto what looks more like a path than a road.

I ask Steve, "Where are we going?" He doesn't answer.

Around a turn in the path is a rounded one-story building, probably built about the time I was born and meant to look futuristic. From behind the building, overshadowing its futuristic ambitions, or perhaps amplifying them, I see a large satellite dish.

Outside the building's front windows and door are signs for

employee parking. I follow the path to the right, around the back of the building, bringing the base of the satellite into view, and around the side, where I see two unmarked parking spaces near a side door.

"Wait," I say to Steve. "I think I remember this."

"Me too," Steve says. "I remember this too."

"What is this?"

"WEEK-TV," Steve says, no coughing. "Where Dad used to take film."

"I remember," I say. "I used to go with him."

"Me too! I used to go with him too!"

The side door to this building seemed so exclusive. It was a special door. Dad would push a button, and someone would open the door to let him in. The door opened into a hallway that looked something like a hospital and something like a spaceship. The person who opened the door would seem happy to see my dad, and I would be greeted too, a greeting just for me. I was impressed with my dad, that he among everyone else in Peoria was allowed to enter this secret place by this secret entrance. Dad would drop off a tin or two of 16-millimeter film, or he would pick up some tins. I knew what was on that film was different than anything being created inside this television station. Here they created the images I saw on television. And yet, I knew the images and movements on the film inside Dad's tins were even more exotic and important.

I stop the car near the unmarked spaces, and Steve and I look at the door.

Back on the road, returning to Peoria, I watch the web of patches on the road, animated by the car's forward motion, wobbling and disappearing beneath me as I drive. I think I would be happy to drive with Steve and to watch these lines for all of the time left in my life.